2/16/60

DATE DUE

MAY 15 '70	
MAY 16 '73	
MAY 19 '75	
SEP 1 3 2004	
OCT 1 1 2004	

The Wonderful World

CONTENTS

The Past Sets a Problem 7

Preserving the Clues 14

Unearthing History 24

Method and Science 46

The Past Has a Future 64

Library of Congress Card Catalog Number 56-10765

Produced by Rathbone Books – London

Printed in Great Britain by L. T. A. Robinson Ltd. – London

# of ARCHAEOLOGY

RONALD JESSUP

Art by
Norman Battershill – Kenneth Symonds
Diagrams by
Isotype Institute

FIRST PUBLISHED IN THE UNITED STATES OF AMERICA 1956

GARDEN CITY BOOKS   GARDEN CITY   NEW YORK

19431

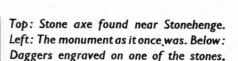

(From Salisbury Museum Model)

(From Salisbury Museum Model)

Top: Stone axe found near Stonehenge.
Left: The monument as it once was. Below:
Daggers engraved on one of the stones.

The Past
Sets a Problem

AMID THE broad expanse of Salisbury Plain, in the west of England, rises a great circle of standing stones called Stonehenge. Who built it? How long ago? What was its purpose? Its builders left no written answers to these questions and for many years people were content to guess. In the Middle Ages writers told fantastic stories of its being moved bodily from Ireland by Merlin, the wizard of Arthurian legend, to serve as a British memorial to warriors killed by the Saxons. During the seventeenth and eighteenth centuries various people thought that it was a Druid's temple, the burial ground of kings, an astronomical observatory, a memorial to the warrior-queen Boadicea, or even, perhaps, the work of the Phoenicians.

Not until the nineteenth and twentieth centuries did archaeologists seriously look in order to learn the facts. Yet some thirty years ago, when more than half the site had already been excavated, the origin and purpose of this remarkable monument were still a mystery.

Since then methods have improved, new scientific techniques have been introduced, and more work has been done on the site. Today, thanks to our new knowledge of radio-activity, we are able to say with some certainty that the first phase of this impressive building operation began between 1900 and 1700 B.C. We also know that some of the stone blocks were transported from south-west Wales, nearly a hundred and fifty miles away. We can picture how Stonehenge looked before it fell into ruin. But there is still much to learn.

This is just one example of the kind of problem which the past has set. The bits and pieces of evidence from which such problems can be solved are sometimes scattered over a wide area, often buried in the soil. The task of finding them, recognising them and fitting them together like the pieces of a jig-saw puzzle, to make a clear and meaningful picture, is the special task of archaeology.

To the archaeologist, objects found in house-like tombs tell of Etruscan life. They explain how the farmer worked, how the army fought.

Let us look at part of the history of one small corner of the world so that we can begin to see how the archaeologist sets to work.

About 800 B.C., before Rome had risen to greatness, the fine Etruscan civilisation appeared suddenly in the north-west of Italy. Where did the Etruscans come from? What kind of people were they? How did they live?

Unlike the builders of Stonehenge they left many writings: some on tombstones, some on cups and vases, and one, strangely enough, preserved in the bindings of an Egyptian mummy. Yet these writings are of less help than we might at first suppose. Although the Etruscans used the same alphabet as the Greeks, they used it to make quite different words, and so far only about a hundred of them have been translated. Further, many Etruscan inscriptions consist of little more than proper names. Some day an inscription may be found which is repeated in Etruscan and some known language, such as Greek. If so, it will give us a key.

Meanwhile the archaeologist depends on other ways of probing the mystery of this great, vanished civilisation. He finds a vase or a gold trinket here, a bronze statuette or a piece of gay and lively wall-painting there, and from a careful study of many such objects, most of them of great beauty and fine workmanship, he gradually builds up a

A terra-cotta head of a god.

picture of the men and women who made and used them. He learns something of their art and religion, of their quest for food, of the shape and condition of their houses and settlements, of how they fought, how they worked, how they spent their leisure.

With the help of photographs taken from the air, he reveals the obliterated sites of long-forgotten roads, and thus learns something of the Etruscans' ability as engineers and organisers. By finding and recognising objects of Etruscan workmanship in other parts of the world, he has learned that this ancient people probably traded with places as far apart as North Africa and Asia Minor.

The archaeologist may also learn something from the works of the classical authors. But here, as in the legend of Horatius holding the bridge single-handed

Wall-paintings bring to life the sportsman and the chase; jewellery and bronze mirrors help the artist to reconstruct domestic scenes.

This painting from a tomb shows the music and feasting which filled a large part of everyday life.

Etruscan beaded gold work.

against Etruscan troops, it is often hard to sift fact from fancy.

Writers of classical times believed that the Etruscans came from Asia Minor, and there is certainly evidence to support that belief. Their religious ceremonies and some of their earliest art show a close likeness to those of certain eastern Mediterranean lands, and the fact that their first settlements were near the coast indicates that they may have arrived by sea. Some authorities, however, still believe that these people were natives of Italy.

Yet, in spite of some remaining doubts, archaeologists are well on the way to completing this corner of the puzzle of the past.

In the first century of the present era, Pompeii was a flourishing Roman city with fine public buildings, shops and large houses.

Death of a city

HOW DID the past become a puzzle? How have the pieces been lost or buried? It has happened in many different ways, but few are more dramatic than the burial of Pompeii.

This fine Roman city was overwhelmed completely in A.D. 79 by the disastrous eruption of the volcano Vesuvius. The historian Pliny the Younger, whose famous uncle witnessed the beginning of the disaster and was finally killed in it, describes how the city was buried deep in a rain of ashes and windborne lava. Many of its inhabitants met their death while fleeing from the terror; others were suffocated in the cellars to which they had run for shelter. Private houses, public buildings, factories and workshops, all were engulfed. But not everything was destroyed; the lava which covered the city also preserved much of what it buried.

The lost Pompeii was first re-discovered more than three hundred years ago – not by archaeologists but by engineers. While digging an underground canal through the soft lava, they uncovered several inscriptions and many houses with walls of brightly painted plaster. There was further digging during the eighteenth century; then in 1860 a systematic plan of work was adopted: quarter by quarter and house by house the town was methodically examined.

Today we can see much of the ancient city of Pompeii almost as its long-dead inhabitants saw it.

Nearby, overlooking the city, was the volcano, Vesuvius.

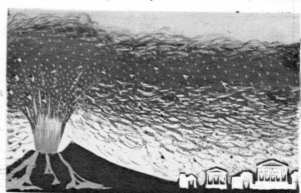
In A.D. 79 it erupted, burying all in ashes and lava.

Slowly vegetation grew up and covered the whole site.

Here are the ovens and mills of a bakery, there a tavern with its pots, hanging lamp and petty cash still in place. Here, again, is preserved the figure of a boy blinded by ashes as, with a little food in a basket, he tried to escape.

We see that in Pompeii, a town of busy commerce and trade, the public buildings are large and impressive. Here are fine places of entertainment, a great amphitheatre for staging events out-of-doors,

Sudden terror brought all life to a dramatic end. The city was overwhelmed. Only a smoking volcano bore witness to the buried past.

and splendid public baths. But it is the simple messages found scratched or painted on the walls which make the ruins of Pompeii so appealing and so at one with our own time: advertisements of all kinds, election slogans, business notes, love notes, shopkeepers' tallies, children's first lessons.

The very calamity which brought death and destruction to the city has, in a sense, made it live on to the present day.

Watch-dog, from a mosaic pavement.

In prehistoric times, the lake-villages of central Europe supported a thriving population with well-developed arts, crafts and husbandry.

Nature has several other ways of burying and thus preserving the past. Most of them are not as sudden as that which engulfed Pompeii, but often they are just as effective.

The dry sands of Egypt overwhelmed the royal tombs in the Valley of the Kings: writings thus preserved on fragile papyrus provide knowledge of the early Egyptians, Greeks and Romans which otherwise would have been lost. In Central Asia, valuable discoveries concerning bygone times have been made in the sand-covered rubbish heaps of a settlement abandoned nearly two thousand years ago. At Skara Brae, in the Orkney Islands, off the north of Scotland, blown sand covered the stone houses of a Neolithic (New Stone Age) village; about a hundred years ago a violent storm uncovered it, complete.

Over the long centuries, land surfaces rise and fall. By the sinking of land in the Alpine regions of Europe, once-flourishing lake-side and lake-island settlements of prehistoric peoples became slowly covered by water and by natural deposits of peat. When, a century ago, an exceptionally dry, cold winter caused lake and river levels to drop, the frames of wooden houses once again came into view, complete in structural details. Not only were the houses revealed, but also examples of food, tools, weapons, wooden utensils, baskets and even textiles. From such evidence, many details of life in Neolithic Europe have been learned. We now know, for instance, that men of the time enjoyed apples and pears, and sprinkled poppy seed on their bread.

Huts on piles stood above water until peat beds raised levels.

Then all trace vanished until a drought revealed their outlines.

Relics of Bronze-
Age lake settlements

Below London's streets are remains of earlier cities. These stone heads come from a Roman temple found under modern buildings.

food. Miners in Alaska and men digging for buried ivory in Siberia often bring such remains to light. From them the archaeologist not only learns more about early man's hunting weapons, but also about his migrations from continent to continent.

In addition to Nature, man himself has been responsible for breaking up and burying the material remains of the past. In times of peace men have often used the stones of ancient monuments to build new houses. In times of war towns may be devastated and never rebuilt: the Hindu battles with the Moslem invader, his cities fall and lie desolate right down to our own time.

In Roman London a great fire lays waste much of the settlement about the River Walbrook: houses collapse into ruin, the rubble of old foundations is levelled up, life begins afresh and new houses are built on the site. The river floods, breaks its course and forms a quagmire. Long after, people of the Middle Ages live and work in the same place, and human settlement continues through peace and war, fire and flood, down to the present day. The ground level has risen continuously until there is now thirty feet of accumulated human history below London's streets.

Man has also broken up the pattern of the past in his roles of collector, hoarder and robber. Valuable antiquities have been moved from place to place at the whim of the souvenir-hunter; the Romans buried the silver of earlier times against the coming of the barbarians; and what more might we now know of the ancient Egyptians had there been no robberies from the treasure-laden tombs of the Pharaohs!

Climate itself is an important factor in the breaking up of the past. Nowhere is this more apparent than in regions of extreme heat and constant heavy rains, where vegetation grows rapidly. Many ancient cities of Indo-China, among them Angkor Thom, with the nearby temple, Angkor Wat, are buried deep in tropical jungles. The deserted Mayan cities of Central America, too, fell century by century into further decay until at last they were covered by a protective mantle of the very jungle which had caused their ruin.

In the other extreme of climate, frozen silts slowly covered the remains of prehistoric man and the now extinct animals which he once hunted for

At Skara Brae, buried stone houses of prehistoric times were revealed by a storm.

From Easter Island, sailors took gigantic stone statues.

The museum label

An antiquity from Bel-Shalti-Nannar's museum

Bel-Shalti-Nannar, a sister of Belshazzar, was not only princess, priestess and antiquary, but also a teacher

Preserving the Clues

WHEN THE THINGS of the past are buried by nature or destroyed by man, the memory of them may easily be lost. But man, like nature, can preserve as well as destroy. In words and in pictures he can capture the living incidents of his own time and leave them on record for future generations.

In ancient Egypt and Mesopotamia, men often left inscriptions on the walls of temples and palaces, recording the circumstances in which they were built; artists and craftsmen also made vivid records of the daily life around them. One famous mosaic from Mesopotamia, the Royal Standard of Ur, clearly pictures the life of a prince, in peace and war, five thousand years ago. But ancient Mesopotamia not only produced recorders of current events; it also produced antiquaries.

Some thirty years ago, while excavating at Ur, where history lies buried layer under layer, Sir Leonard Woolley made a remarkable discovery. On the floor of a room built about 550 B.C. for the use of Princess Bel-Shalti-Nannar, sister of Belshazzar, he found objects dating back to 1400 B.C., 1700 B.C., and 2050 B.C. How could these things have strayed from older layers, near the bottom of the excavation, to the highest and most recent level? Fortunately Woolley found the answer. Nearby was a drum-shaped clay tablet bearing copies of very ancient inscriptions, together with an original inscription made only a century or so before the time of the Princess. The last one explained how the earlier inscriptions had been found and copied out 'for the marvel of beholders'. It was, in fact, one of the world's earliest museum

Egyptian statue of about 600 B.C., carved in style of a far earlier period.

The Ziggurat of Ur, as it was in the days of Nabonidus, last king of Babylon.

The Ziggurat as Ur-Nammu built it, 1500 years earlier.

The Standard of Ur, a record in mosaic of life 5000 years ago.

labels; the room itself was a museum, and Bel-Shalti-Nannar was a collector of antiquities.

Her father, King Nabonidus, shared his love of the past. In repairing Ur's great Ziggurat, or 'Hill of Heaven', he carefully noted that the original building was erected by a much earlier king, Ur-Nammu. He also expressed keen pleasure at finding a foundation tablet in an ancient temple.

In Egypt, too, there were kings with similar tastes. About 700 B.C., King Shabaka ordered that the writings on a worm-eaten document, already two thousand years old, should be copied in stone. A century later, under King Psammetichus, many statues were carved in styles of far earlier times.

The Father of Archaeology

Delphi was widely known in ancient Greece for the famous Oracle of Apollo.

The greatest of all antiquaries of long ago was Herodotus, born of a well-to-do family at Halicarnassus, in Asia Minor, in the fifth century B.C. Perhaps his love of the past was inspired by reading the old heroic stories of the Iliad and the Odyssey.

As a young man he travelled widely in western Greece, Asia Minor and Syria, visiting many of the places that figured in those stories. Later he saw lands that were the homes of earlier civilisations: Egypt, Mesopotamia and the northern coast of the Black Sea. He visited famous cities such as Babylon, Tyre and Ecbatana, capital of the Medes. He saw the great pyramids, and was acquainted with many prophecies of the Oracle of Delphi.

On his journeys he seized every opportunity of learning all he could about the history and people of the places he passed through. Often he stayed for some time, making careful notes from first-hand observations, recording conversations, measuring old monuments, enquiring about the people who built them, and about anything else which engaged his inquisitive mind.

Eventually, the fruits of his work and travels were embodied in a long book which began with these words: This is the History of Herodotus of Halicarnassus, published in order that what has happened may not be forgotten of men by the passing of time. . . . Then, against a background of the history of Persia, the lands it had conquered and its wars with Greece, Herodotus set down all he had seen and heard.

In Egypt Herodotus visited pyramids and temples, observing and listening to gossip.

Moated walls and temple of mighty Babylon.

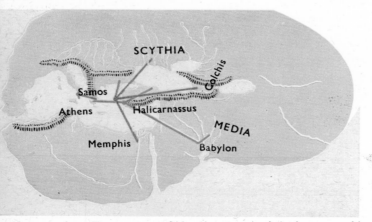

The journeys of Herodotus covered the known world.

First
Second
Third

Alexandria, a thriving port, was also a great home of learning. Its famous libraries enshrined a vast knowledge of the past.

The result was a history of the greater part of the then-known world. Not only did he describe the people themselves, their work and play, their customs and their legends, but also the geography of their countries with special reference to antiquities. In his own lifetime, his writings were made known to a wide audience by means of public readings. Today, his *History* is often regarded as the first great prose work in European literature, and Herodotus himself as the Father of Archaeology. (The word archaeology comes from two Greek words which together mean discussion

The Persian Wars shown on a Greek pottery bowl.

of the past.) In original and in translation, his famous work has been passed down from generation to generation, and is still read with interest and enjoyment. But not all written history of this period shared the same fortune.

In 332 B.C., a century after the death of Herodotus, the fine city of Alexandria, named after Alexander the Great, was founded. It very soon became not only a busy trading port, but also a unique storehouse of learning. Ships of many lands brought merchandise to its warehouses, scholars from far and wide studied in, and added to, its vast library. At its height, this famous library contained no less than 700,000 scrolls. Had they survived to our own time they would have added immeasurably to our knowledge of the past. But in 145 B.C. riots and civil war destroyed a great part of the library. The destruction was completed about 47 B.C., when Julius Caesar was blockaded in the city. A new library later arose and amassed a smaller collection of scrolls, but centuries after, these too suffered the same fate. Thus part of the history of the civilisations of Greek and Roman times, formerly preserved in writing, was lost.

In the fifth century the already-declining power of Rome was finally broken when the Eternal City was sacked by barbarian invaders.

Chronicles of the Church

Some four centuries after Alexandria fell to the power of Rome, the mighty Roman Empire itself began to totter. Already diminished in size, already split into an eastern and a western half, already hard pressed by dissatisfied non-Roman troops inside its own borders, it fell a surprisingly easy prey to the onslaught of invading barbarians.

At its height, the Empire of Rome, stretching from the Atlantic Ocean to the Persian Gulf and from Scotland to the south of Egypt, had given men a sense of belonging to a large, closely-knit world. Its long, unbroken history, reaching back through time to the last glories of ancient Greece, Persia and Egypt, had also built up among the peoples of Europe and the Near East a strong sense of one-ness with the past.

When the Roman Empire fell, the peoples of Europe, both east and west, soon lost the old sense of unity. The Byzantine part of the Empire, around Constantinople (now Istanbul), where men were surrounded by so many buildings and monuments of earlier times, kept much of its feeling of being linked to the past. But Western Europe, cut off from the homelands of early civilisations, soon found the link of history weakening.

Yet even there, some memories of antiquity still survived. Late in its history, Imperial Rome had adopted Christianity as its religion, and when Rome fell, the scholars and monks of the Christian Church preserved at least a little of the learning embodied in the works of earlier Greek, Latin and Hebrew writers. St. Augustine, who lived in North Africa at the time of the sack of Rome, wrote much that helped to keep alive the thought and teaching of the great Greek philosopher, Plato. St. Jerome, the first scholar of his age, who died in A.D. 420, not only translated the Bible into Latin for the first time, but also wrote a book from which many later chroniclers formed their idea of history.

For several centuries, the Bible and the works of a handful of early Christian scholars formed almost the only written sources of Western Europe's knowledge of antiquity. In an age when few people could read and fewer still could write, even that knowledge seldom extended far beyond the walls of monasteries. As the centuries passed, monk after monk wrote and re-wrote the story of past times – just as they drew and re-drew maps – with little or no reliable new information to help them, and often calling upon imagination and tradition to fill the gaps.

The maps of the Middle Ages, unlike those of ancient Greece, were not intended to set out hard facts about geography; they were rather the means by which the map-maker expressed his hopes and fears, his religious beliefs and his imaginings about

From Greek, Hebrew and Latin sources, St. Jerome and other churchmen preserved some knowledge of the past.

(After Dürer)

a world of which he knew little. In a similar way, the medieval historian, while a careful chronicler of his own times, could seldom set down established facts about the ancient past. Instead, he described what he felt should have been, or what he thought might have been. So few pieces from the true picture of the past remained in Western Europe, that men had practically given up the attempt to fit them together.

Without facts to guide them, they painted a new picture of history which, quite unavoidably, bore very little likeness to the reality.

Medieval maps, though ingenious, were no guide to the traveller.

20

From Bible stories men gained some knowledge of people and places of bygone ages.

WHAT, we may wonder, did the world look like to the medieval monks whose lovely hand-illuminated manuscripts so often depict such strange and moving combinations of incidents from various books of the Bible?

The Bible gave them, in the form of a simple, vivid story, an account of the world's creation and the beginning of the human race; it also gave them the hope of eternal life when life on earth ended. The Garden of Eden and the Gates of Heaven represented the beginning and end of man's journey through life. That journey, leading to an everlasting future, was man's first business. To the monk of the Middle Ages, the importance of the past lay in the fact that it often carried a message which might help to sustain men on the road.

Many books of the Bible, including Genesis, Exodus, Joshua and Samuel, told in simple narrative form how nations, tribes and individual men and women of the past had taken part in the age-old battle between good and evil. By reading such books, scholarly men became familiar with the names of many great cities and countries of old and with the nature of important events of bygone times. They knew the names of Babylon, Nineveh, Tyre and Sidon; they knew something about the building of the Tower of Babel, the siege of Jerusalem, and the destruction of the walls of Jericho. Their knowledge, it is true, was neither deep nor detailed; but the stories of the Old and New Testaments undoubtedly kept alive a real, though limited, interest in the past and its traditions.

Other stories of early times were also known to the Western world: for instance, the story of the founding of Rome; of the wooden horse of Troy; of Alexander's great conquests; of the threat to sacrifice Iphigenia, Agammemnon's daughter, to propitiate the winds that had left the Greek fleet becalmed and helpless.

But, scattered here and there, were other and more powerful reminders of the past: Roman villas and viaducts, triumphal arches and memorial columns which still remained more or less intact. In Rome, for example, was the magnificent column erected by the Senate to commemorate the Emperor Trajan. With its great spiral of carvings representing Trajan's victories, it must always have been

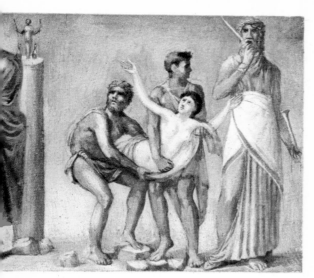

Threatened sacrifice of Iphigenia. (From Pompeii mural)

regarded, by the citizens of Rome and the many pilgrims who visited the city, as an historical document in stone.

In eleventh-century Britain, monks of St. Albans, seeking stone to repair their fine abbey, found it by excavating on the site of the Roman town of Verulamium, nearby. Their careful record of Roman inscriptions, glass and pottery shows that they had a lively interest in antiquity. A century or so later, other excavations were made by the monks of Glastonbury. They found human bones and a lead cross inscribed with the name of King Arthur. For centuries afterwards these finds were believed to prove beyond doubt that Arthur, hero of so many British legends, had once really lived.

Interest in the past was certainly alive, but it was still limited to the monk and the privileged scholar. Ordinary people had very little share in it until the crusades – the Holy Wars in which men from all parts of Europe banded together to wrest Jerusalem from the hands of the Moslems.

Trajan's Column, which carries reliefs showing the Emperor's victories, was probably known to be history carved in stone.

Monks of Glastonbury found what they thought was the grave of Arthur, England's hero-king.

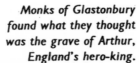

22

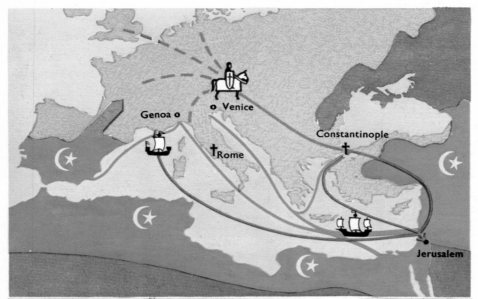

Crusaders, merchants and the teachers of Spain carried Eastern knowledge to Europe.

Western men began to buy oriental luxuries.

Slowly the crusaders re-established the contacts with the past which their ancestors had lost. The prolonged wars took them to ports which had flourished in Greek and Phoenician times, and to the lands of the Bible stories. Their very castles were sometimes built from the stones of Roman walls. Chroniclers who accompanied them kept journals as they moved from one sacred place to another.

At the time of the crusades, knowledge of past civilisations was also moving westward, by other routes and in other ways.

The Moslem Empire, reaching from Portugal to Persia, was founded at a time when many of the writings of early Greek scholars were still preserved in eastern Mediterranean lands. Moslem scholars translated Greek writings on astronomy, geography, medicine and geometry into Arabic, and advanced these studies considerably in their universities. Several of the most famous of the Moslem universities were in Spain, at Cordova, Salamanca and other large towns. They attracted many Jewish and a few Christian students from other parts of Western Europe. These students often took back new knowledge to their own countries, thus helping to stimulate a revival of learning.

During the three centuries that followed the close of the Holy Wars, the outlook of Western Europe steadily broadened. Contacts with the East continued to grow. New fruits, spices, precious stones, exotic fashions, richly figured silks and all kinds of luxuries never before known came by sea from Asia into the ports of Venice and Genoa and moved overland

From Venice, gateway to Asia, ships sailed as far as the Indies.
(Based on fifteenth-century manuscript, Bodleian Library, Oxford)

northward and westward. Men learned of other ways of life and other ways of thinking. New arts and crafts began to flourish. European women saw themselves for the first time in glass mirrors.

The learning of the ancients, kept alive through the Dark Ages inside the Moslem Empire, flourished anew and quickened men's desire to know more of the world and its wonders. Seamen, equipped with

A search for a new route to the East opened up the New World. The art and buildings of Central America spoke of man's long development there.

new navigational instruments and knowing more of astronomy and geography than ever before, were ready and anxious to undertake voyages in search of new lands and new sea-routes to the Indies.

It was in search of such a sea-route that Columbus paved the way for the opening-up of the Americas. This great turning-point in history placed Europe mid-way between the ancient civilisations of the Old World and the future civilisation still to arise in the New. But, from the point of view of man's awareness of the past, it did even more. Only a few years after Columbus first crossed the Atlantic, other travellers began to realise that America itself already had many chapters to add to human history. Buildings of great size, tools of fine workmanship, skilful carvings, all spoke of a long period of development among the native peoples of Central America.

No wonder that Western men, who had so long lost a clear vision of the past, now began to realise its fascination and to take a keener interest in it than they had ever taken before.

An Aztec mosaic mask made of jade and turquoise

Noblemen of Florence adorned their palaces with fine examples of ancient art.

Unearthing History

THE AGE that witnessed the opening-up of the New World, often called the Renaissance, was a time of great opportunity and rapid progress. The breakdown of the old feudal system had given men a new freedom of thought and action; printing, which developed faster, perhaps, than any craft previously known, quickly helped to spread new knowledge and bold philosophies; expanding world-trade brought opportunities of wealth and leisure to a fast-growing merchant class.

The wealthy landowner of the Middle Ages was often unable to read or write, but the merchant-princes of the Renaissance were proud to be counted amongst men of learning, as patrons of science or the arts. Many, conscious of their debt to antiquity, were beginning to enrich their reading of Greek and Roman history by collecting about them the finest examples of classical art. Thus written history began to take on a new significance.

In Florence, when the great Medici family was at the height of its power, the discovery of an ancient manuscript was considered only less important than the acquisition of a province. Cosimo de Medici (1389–1464) ornamented his sumptuous palace with many precious pieces of ancient art, a unique collection of marble statues, pottery, glass vases, gems, coins and medals. Among the statues which Ferdinand de Medici (1549–1609) assembled at his villa in Rome, one, at least, came from the home of the Roman Emperor, Hadrian. Some

The famous Venus de Medici

Here pillars from an ancient temple form part of a later building.

Enthusiasm for the glories of Greece and Rome was fashionable in eighteenth-century England. The wealthy collected antiquities in homes modelled on classical styles.

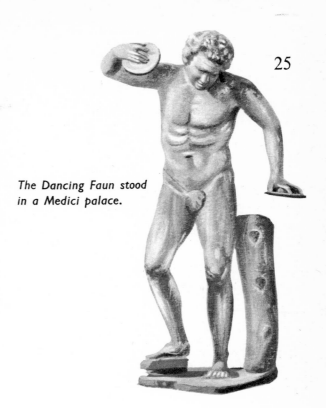

The Dancing Faun stood in a Medici palace.

The Wrestlers: marble copy of bronze statue of third century B.C.

Statue of Niobe with her youngest daughter

of the many treasures of statuary which the Medici family collected are shown on this page.

Two hundred years later, gentlemen of means were still keen collectors. It was fashionable for those who could afford it to make a prolonged tour of Europe, as a means of completing their education, and often such men brought back antiquities from Greece and Italy to beautify their homes or their estates. Relics were no longer quite so easily found lying on the ground as they had been when the

collection of antiquities began; but men were by now learning to dig for the past and even to search for the remains of ancient buildings within the structure of modern ones.

In Britain, and in North-West Europe generally, appreciation of classical times showed itself in the building of the great houses, which were commonly modelled on Roman-Italian (Palladian) styles of architecture; in America, particularly in the north-eastern States, interest in the past played a part in the naming of such towns as Ithaca, Marathon, Homer, Troy, and Carthage.

Yet interest in bygone times was by no means confined to Greece and Rome. The man who brought back relics from his Grand Tour was becoming equally ready to search for antiquities beneath the soil of his own estate. There was a growing realisation that almost every nook and corner of the world held evidence of the vast panorama of man's story.

As yet there was nothing approaching skilled excavation, but people were fast realising that history was not confined entirely to books. Much of it was buried beneath their feet.

The fashion of studying history in the open air spread: digging for the past became a popular pastime. Digging led to writing and discussion. Many books were published, many antiquarian societies formed. It was not long before the man of wealth and culture ceased to be a mere collector of curios, and became an amateur of archaeology.

The Acropolis, seat of the temples and sanctuaries of ancient Athens.

This was an important landmark in the history of archaeology – the first organised expedition.

Many other travellers, inspired by this example, and after studying the works of classical Greek historians, wrote entertainingly of their own travels in search of the grand and the picturesque in Greece. Collectors of antiquities of all kinds set to work on a really large scale. Outstanding among these was Lord Elgin, who was appointed British Ambassador to Turkey in 1799, at a time when Turkish territory included much of the area which was formerly the homeland of Greek civilisation.

The Agora Gate at Athens at the time Stuart and Revett saw it. Turkish mosques stood side by side with buildings of classical times.

Prominent among the antiquarian societies of the eighteenth century was the Society of Dilettanti, formed in London in 1733 to discuss the Mediterranean journeys of its members and to encourage good taste among collectors of antiquities.

Towards the middle of the century, James Stuart, an English artist, and his architect friend Revett, spent three years in Athens, copying inscriptions, making drawings, and carefully recording the outstanding ancient monuments of the city. Later their work was published by the Dilettanti, and so much interest did it arouse that within a short time after the publication appeared the Society decided to send out an Ionic Expedition.

From the Turkish government he received a permit to remove carved figures from the Parthenon. This temple had been bombarded more than a century earlier, and many such works were still lying on the ground. Under Elgin's direction two hundred cases of marble sculptures were collected and sent to England. After some years of neglect they were eventually bought by the British government and today the Elgin Marbles are still a highly valued possession of the British Museum. It was after seeing them that Keats wrote his famous "Ode on a Grecian Urn".

From 1821 to 1832 the Greeks waged a long War of Independence against the Turks, which resulted in the setting-up of an independent Greek kingdom. Travel and archaeological exploration now became easier, and soon other countries began to send expeditions to Greece and its islands.

By 1829 the French were excavating works of art from the ruins of Olympia, which had played so large a part in Greek sport, religion and politics. Some ten years later the Germans began work at Delphi, the site of the Oracle of Apollo, below the peaks of Parnassus.

Temples and tombs, public buildings and private houses all came under the scrutiny of the archaeologists. Towns were cleared of rubbish, shrines and treasuries explored. Marble sculptures of incomparable beauty, such as the Winged Victory of Samothrace, several fine statues of Venus, the Charioteer of Delphi, and the Hermes of Praxiteles, became famous the world over. The everyday life of ancient Greece became known as it had not been for the past fifteen hundred years. Excavation was making it possible to add to, and sometimes even to re-write, history.

Throughout the nineteenth century, almost every civilised nation of the world – not least the Greek people themselves – took part in unearthing the dramatic story of this ancient land. Thus Greece, which gave us the Father of Archaeology was also the land where modern archaeology served its

Finding a statue of Hadrian's favourite, Antinous, at Delphi.

apprenticeship. There, within little more than a century, unearthing history changed from a collector's hobby into a serious and systematic study. Finding antiquities was no longer the sole purpose: increasing knowledge of man and his story was now the main quest.

But, as we have already noticed, while the picture of Greece was still being revealed, interest in the past was steadily widening in other directions. The techniques of excavation, of drawing, and recording which archaeologists first used there were already being applied elsewhere. Not only the lands of the eastern Mediterranean but also those of Central America were beginning to yield up the hidden secrets of their long, eventful histories.

The famous Elgin Marbles, two of which are shown below, were obtained from the Parthenon.

British Museum

The Agora Gateway as it is today – preserved amid modern Athens

Catherwood's drawing of a Mayan stele from Stephens's book on Central America.

SHEER chance took a hand in the beginning of archaeology in the New World. John Lloyd Stephens, born in 1805 in Shrewsbury, New Jersey, became in course of time a busy lawyer with little time for his hobby – the study of antiquities. When he found himself suffering with throat trouble he welcomed his doctor's suggestion of a tour in the Mediterranean and Eastern Europe. The result was two travel-books, works which quickly became classics of their kind.

Back home, in 1839, Stephens was delighted when the President sent him on a diplomatic mission to Central America. He was already familiar with the works of Dupaix and de Waldeck, who a few years earlier had written accounts of this area; he also knew of an early eighteenth-century traveller's story of strange and very old buildings which were to be found in the depths of the Honduras jungle.

His chosen travelling companion was an Englishman, Frederick Catherwood, an accomplished artist with much experience of drawing ancient buildings. They made an ideal pair. Willingly they journeyed all over Guatemala seeking the government to which Stephens was said to be accredited but which he could never find.

The nightmare journey was beset with difficulties. The countryside was in revolt, food was scarce, and the Indians unfriendly. All around was the green wilderness of the jungle, impenetrable until a way had been cleared with an axe. Mules and baggage sank deep in muddy swamps; thorn bushes and mosquitoes made progress wearying.

Stephens buys a city.

Archaeology has made it possible for artists to reconstruct such grand buildings as the Mayan Temple of the Warriors at Chichen-Itzà.

Yet the two men persisted until at last, at Copan in Honduras, they saw, covered by jungle-growth, a long flight of stone steps. Hacking vines and tree-roots as they went, they climbed the steps and came out on to a wall and a broad terrace hidden by centuries of tree-growth. The explorers had found a temple of the ancient Mayas. They did not know when or by whom it was built; nor did the Indian who owned the building. Never having seen

Catherwood records the jungle-hidden past.

the ancient city which stood on his estate, he sold the whole site to Stephens for a mere fifty dollars.

On his return, Stephens published a book about his travels. Illustrated with Catherwood's fine and detailed drawings, carefully made on the spot, it was translated into several languages and excited keen interest, both in the New World and the Old.

Many people turned once more to the records of early Spanish settlers who had written with first-hand knowledge of the old civilisations of Central America; others took up the work of exploration and rediscovery which Stephens had begun.

In the light of modern knowledge, the conclusions which Stephens drew are no longer accepted, but his keen observation made him the real founder of Mayan archaeology. Had it not been for the New York lawyer with his sore throat such a reconstruction of a Mayan temple as shown here might not have been possible for many years.

High on the Rock of Behistun was carved the clue to a lost language.

While Mayan archaeology was still in its early infancy, the story of a far older civilisation was being unravelled in Western Asia.

Mesopotamia, the land between the Rivers Euphrates and Tigris, was by tradition regarded as the site of the Garden of Eden. There, between the Mediterranean and the Persian Gulf, astride the chief trade-route of the ancient world, great and famous empires once flourished. Of the cities of those empires nothing remained but mysterious flat-topped mounds in the desert.

There were no visible remains of temples and palaces to appeal to the imagination and set people working on a thorough search. But from the sixteenth century onwards, occasional European travellers had brought home odd curios: tablets of clay inscribed in a strange wedge-shaped script.

A German college-lecturer named Grotefend had begun to decipher the ancient scripts of Mesopotamia as early as 1802, but his work did not gain much recognition until years afterwards. The most spectacular part in the decipherment was played, some forty years later, by the British orientalist, Sir Henry Rawlinson.

Working precariously, far above ground-level, he and his native helpers made careful copies of ancient inscriptions carved on a rock at Behistun, in Persia. These inscriptions carried the same message in three different languages – Old Persian, Elamite and Babylonian. Starting from a few royal titles known in Old Persian, it was possible for Rawlinson to work backwards to an understanding of the older,

Before the task of decipherment came the dangers of recording.

but related, scripts. In this way a key was provided which, soon after serious excavation began, was to unlock a vast storehouse of knowledge about the cradle of civilisation.

In 1842 a French physician, turned diplomat, became the pioneer of excavation in Mesopotamia – a work which was to continue for more than a century. Through the memorable explorations of Paul Botta, which were officially supported by the French government, the world first began to add to its meagre knowledge of these ancient lands. It was Botta who, from the long-buried palace of an Assyrian king, unearthed the magnificent stone sculptures and relief carvings which now form a famous exhibition in the Louvre, in Paris.

Meanwhile, Austen Henry Layard, an Englishman whose early dreams of the East were influenced by

Arabs guard the Black Obelisk during one stage of its journey to England.

The Obelisk records in script and sculpture events of almost 3000 years ago.

(From an engraving)

Excited Arabs uncover an enormous head carved out of stone.

the stories of the *Arabian Nights*, made his second journey to Mesopotamia with the object of excavating the mound of Nimrud. With the help of a few Arabs he was at once successful. First Layard noticed a single large slab of stone; by the end of a morning's work he had found a whole room. Success followed success, and in time the mound was found to cover the palaces of three Assyrian kings who had ruled at different periods between 883 and 669 B.C. As Layard's work progressed, several priceless treasures, now housed in the British Museum, were revealed – a black stone obelisk recording in script and sculpture the main events of the reign of King Shalmaneser III (858–828 B.C.); giant winged bulls carved out of stone; enormous sculptures of human-headed lions.

During another expedition Layard discovered the palace of King Sennacherib with its great library of clay tablets. The work of the decipherers made it possible to read what proved to be prayers, incantations, stories, scientific texts, legal reports and official letters, all of which shed new light on one small corner of human history.

Visitors to the British Museum first saw this huge Assyrian sculpture over a century ago.

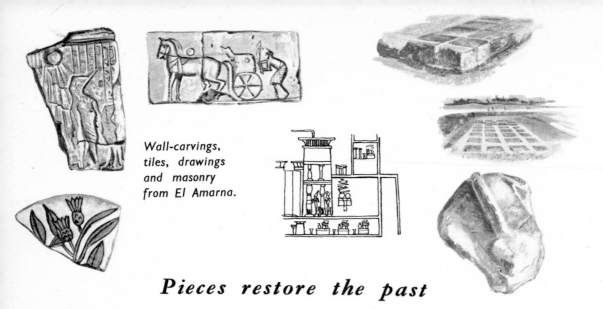

Wall-carvings, tiles, drawings and masonry from El Amarna.

A temple of Akhenaten's fine city, El Amarna.

Pieces restore the past

The old civilisations of the Nile valley were never forgotten as completely as those of Mesopotamia: throughout the ages they have proclaimed their grandeur through the Sphinx, the pyramids, and the ruins of mighty temples rising from the sands. Yet it was not until the end of the eighteenth century that everyday life in ancient Egypt began to be understood. Here, too, an inscription in three languages provided one of the main clues.

In his expedition to Egypt in 1798, Napoleon Bonaparte included among his army geographers, scientists and skilled draughtsmen whose duty it was to collect and study antiquities. Nothing they found was to prove as important as the Rosetta Stone. This stone repeated a royal decree in hieroglyphic, in a script called Demotic, and in Greek. From the known Greek the two unknown scripts were deciphered, and in time many written records of Egypt were made plain.

By the middle of the nineteenth century much of the history of the Nile valley was known. Archaeologists from France, Britain, the Netherlands, Italy, and Germany all made contributions, especially in decipherment. Thousands of papyri which had formerly seemed meaningless now told of the arts and crafts, the customs and beliefs, the kings, priests and prophets of long past ages. The chief monuments of ancient Egypt had always been familiar; but now the inscriptions they bore told of their purpose and of the men who built them. Nor was it only through writing that the past spoke to the present. Carvings, paintings, decorated tiles and even models which had been placed in the tombs of kings and rulers all added vividly to the message.

From scraps of paintings an artist depicts life in the women's quarters of a palace.

The Rosetta Stone, the key to much of Egypt's written history, was found during one of Napoleon's campaigns.

Models from tombs tell of life and work in ancient Egypt.
British Museum

Diplomatic letters

From a reconstruction made for the Egypt Exploration Society.

Workmen's houses as well as temples were excavated at El Amarna.

Often archaeologists concentrated on one small area of promise. Such an area was the site of El Amarna, some two hundred miles south of Cairo. This once-great city was founded in 1375 B.C. by the Pharaoh Akhenaten who, by his attempt to introduce a new religion of one god, had brought down on himself the wrath of the priests. El Amarna was occupied only until a short time after the king's death and then abandoned. Slowly the shifting tide of sand overwhelmed it.

In 1888 a peasant woman digging on the site for decayed brickwork to use as fertiliser unearthed hundreds of inscribed clay tablets. Before their importance had been realised, many of them were destroyed or lost. But those which survived were found to be the diplomatic letters of long-dead Egyptians, giving a dramatic account of the fall of an empire.

Ten years later Sir Flinders Petrie discovered at El Amarna the famous painted pavements of the harem of the Great Palace. In the years which followed, the Deutsche Orient-Gesellschaft, a German archaeological society, and the Egypt Exploration Society, a British organisation, continued work on the site of the city. Their finds included a sculptor's studio, the beautifully sculptured head of Nefertiti (Akhenaten's wife), and examples of the oldest known glass-work of any size in the world. Yet because of their value in revealing the past, the less spectacular discoveries were sometimes even more important: foundations of buildings, drawings, broken bits of masonry and scraps of painted tiles.

From such evidence it is now possible to picture some of the temples and other great buildings of El Amarna as Akhenaten saw them.

Noting the details of the painted pavement.

Egyptian glass vase　　　*British Museum*

Schliemann's first sight of the hill beneath which lay the city of his boyhood dreams.

A legend comes to life

UNEARTHING buried cities has not always been accomplished by archaeologists with a lifetime of study and training. In one very famous case it was the work of a man who began business life in a shop.

Heinrich Schliemann was born in 1822 at Schwerin in Mecklenburg, North Germany, the son of a poor pastor who took a keen interest in ancient history. When he was only seven years old, his father gave him a book containing a striking picture of Aeneas fleeing from the horrors of burning Troy. From that time on, Troy became an obsession with him. He found it almost impossible to believe that this once-powerful city had vanished, without leaving so much as a clue to its whereabouts.

At Hissarlik nine settlements were buried, one below another.

Most educated people of the day regarded the old Homeric stories of Troy as no more than pleasing legends, for even Herodotus had found no trace of the city, and learned men simply could not believe it had ever really existed. Yet what others regarded as legend, Schliemann accepted as fact. To find the lost city of Troy became the ruling passion of his singularly adventurous life.

It was an ambition not easily to be realised. There was no money in the family to provide him with a classical education, and the dreamer of Troy became first a grocer's apprentice and then a cabin-boy. After suffering ship-wreck off the Dutch coast he settled down as a book-keeper to a firm in Amsterdam where, in an amazingly short time, he mastered seven or eight foreign languages. His knowledge of Russian led to an appointment in St. Petersburg (now Leningrad), and by 1847 Schliemann was already his own master. Thenceforth his career was marked by one success after another. His various enterprises took him to the United States, where he acquired American citizenship, then to Egypt, Greece, Palestine and Syria. Wherever he went he was quick to seize business opportunities, and at the age of forty-one he retired a very wealthy man.

In 1868, after a period of archaeological study in Paris and a spell of world travel, Schliemann at last set out to search for Troy. The few people who

A battle of Trojan times, as portrayed on a Greek vase.

believed that the city really had existed thought it must have stood near a village named Bunarbashi, in Asia Minor, but Schliemann, relying on Homer, sought it nearer the coast. With the help of a guide he came upon a flat-topped mound called Hissarlik, which seemed to him to fit Homer's description of the city's position.

There, for several seasons and with a hundred workmen to help him, he went to work. At the end of his digging, when he struck bedrock, he had laid bare the remains of nine successive decayed and buried cities, one below another. None had previously been known, and Schliemann, discoverer of Homeric Greece, became world-famous. On the very day before work was due to cease, he and his Greek wife came upon priceless gold treasures that had lain hidden since before the days of Troy.

On catching sight of the first gleam of gold, nearly thirty feet below ground, Schliemann sent away all his helpers. Only he and his wife remained, frenziedly cutting ancient gold from beneath an ancient wall, heedless of the danger of falling masonry; and together they smuggled out of the country a treasure of great historical value as well as of gold.

Although Schliemann was mistaken as to which of his nine cities was Homer's Troy, the grocer's boy had nevertheless added a thousand years to history.

On the very day before digging was due to end, Schliemann and his Greek wife discovered a hoard of gold, buried thousands of years ago.

National Museum, Athens

Ornaments, bracelet, necklace, mask – a small part of the treasure.

Digging for prehistory began before excavation became a science.

Primitive implements brought up by the dredger set Boucher de Perthes studying early man. Above are some tools he later excavated.

The century in which Schliemann lived witnessed a revolution in ideas about man's place in a past far more distant than that of Troy.

It began with a renewed interest in old reports of stone tools which had been discovered near the remains of extinct animals, deep down in cave deposits. Knowing approximately how long nature takes to build up such deposits, geologists realised that these remains belonged to a very remote period indeed. Here was a new field of study: that of men who had lived before history began.

Digging for prehistory began before excavation became a science.

One of the leaders in the study of pre-history was Boucher de Perthes, a French customs officer who became interested in antiquities thrown up during the dredging of the Somme Canal. About 1837 he turned his attention to the local gravel pits where he found many hundreds of flaked flint axes, and with them the bones of reindeer, bears, and the long-extinct mammoth.

By 1859, after a prolonged period of doubt, the learned world accepted his discoveries as authentic: de Perthes had proved that man existed far longer ago than had previously been believed.

Meanwhile, knowledge of early man had been greatly furthered by a Dane named Christian J. Thomsen who, in 1819, became curator of the Danish National Museum. Interested in antiquities since his early boyhood, Thomsen now shared his enthusiasm with visitors to the museum, and especially with country folk who, in their work on the land, might well unearth further evidence of early man. But his most important work was the classification of prehistoric implements according to the materials from which they were made. His theory that a Stone Age, a Bronze Age, and an Iron Age mark three successive stages in man's development was to become a cornerstone of archaeology. The theory was proved sound by excavation, and thenceforward gave a rough-and-ready guide to the comparative age of prehistoric tools and weapons.

The man who perhaps more than anyone else helped to place the study of prehistory on a scientific basis was the British Army officer, General Pitt-Rivers. He was, even recently, described as the greatest of all archaeological excavators. An investigation into the history of the rifle, undertaken during

Stone Age: Tools made by chipping and grinding stone to give an edge.

Bronze Age: Copper smelted, mixed with tin, and cast in moulds.

Iron Age: Ore smelted, solid metal heated, then hammered to shape.

In Denmark, Thomsen encouraged peasants to bring him any finds which might add to knowledge of the Stone, Bronze and Iron Ages.

his time in the army, led Pitt-Rivers to an interest in the evolution of tools, boats, dress, and all kinds of weapons. In 1880, when he inherited a fortune and a large estate in the west of England, he began a series of skilled excavations of prehistoric and Roman villages, forts and burial grounds, which became models for all future work of this kind.

Always he insisted on great care and precision: exact three-dimensional records must be kept, even to the point of boredom, to ensure that everything he found could be reconstructed on paper. For him a photograph of a skull was not sufficient for the records: he invented an instrument called a craniometer with which he could measure such finds, with great exactness, at many different angles.

By such painstaking and methodical work he was able to throw much new light on primitive men, their appearance, their possessions, and the way they lived. He was also, perhaps, the first archaeologist to realise that, in recreating the past, the humble and ordinary things may count every bit as much as the grand and impressive ones.

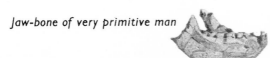

Jaw-bone of very primitive man

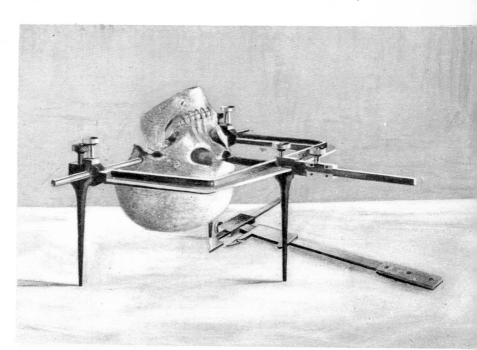

Pitt-Rivers used the craniometer to measure skulls accurately.

Recent excavation of a prehistoric site in northern Algeria.

The Golden Throne of King Tutankhamun

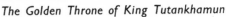

Model boat made of calcite

Headlines for a Pharaoh

During the nineteenth century, the man in the street was already getting to know about the work of archaeologists, but not until the nineteen-twenties did he share the thrill of a great discovery.

To Dr. Howard Carter, the discovery of the tomb of the youthful Pharaoh, Tutankhamun, was the climax of six seasons of carefully-planned though unrewarded work. To the public it was a sensational news-item, proclaimed in bold headlines and broadcast from the newly-opened radio stations. Backed by Lord Carnarvon, an enlightened patron, and eagerly followed by representatives of the world's press, Carter popularised archaeology as had never been done before.

He had abandoned the old method of excavation and replaced it with the then novel idea of digging down to the solid rock, so as to uncover every possible feature of archaeological interest. In the side of a small hillock, he at last found sixteen steps leading down to what he knew must be a tomb. Below was a heavily plastered door bearing the seals of King Tutankhamun.

Within was an antechamber, filled to overflowing with a mass of decorated boxes, vases, statues and royal furniture, and even the king's throne. This room was just as the tomb-robbers had left it many centuries before. Beyond were two other sealed chambers. The larger, opened with great ceremonial in 1923, housed the golden shrine of the king. Here, later, was seen the royal mummy, enclosed within three coffins. The inner one, of solid gold, needed eight men to lift it. As sheer bullion its value is enormous, but as a work of art, it is beyond price, a great masterpiece of the goldsmith's craft.

An adjoining treasury contained untold wealth. As Carter gazed spellbound through the doorway,

As Carter gazed spellbound through the doorway he saw, guarded by the jackal-headed god Anubis, the rich treasury of the young Pharaoh.

Bringing to the outer world the fragile relics
of a king who reigned from 1357 to 1349 B.C.

Inside the tomb, Carter found three coffins, one within another.
The third, of solid gold, held the embalmed body of Tutankhamun.

he saw, guarded by a statue of the god Anubis, the
richly decorated shrine containing the king's organs,
removed by the embalmers when the body was
prepared for burial. Near by were the king's
chariots, his hunting bow, his personal jewels, and
even his sandals. Here, too, were statues of
guardian gods; little effigies of servants of the dead
to do the king's will in the afterworld; models of a
granary and a mill, to supply his food; model ships
in which he could follow the voyages of the sun
across the heavens.

Why did Carter's discovery fire popular imagination the world over? Much was already known about
other Egyptian kings far more powerful than
Tutankhamun. Yet here, for the very first time,
was revealed the full splendour of an Egyptian
royal burial; now, at last, men of our own age could
gaze on the face of a long-dead Pharaoh.

The innermost coffin – a
masterpiece of the goldsmith's craft.

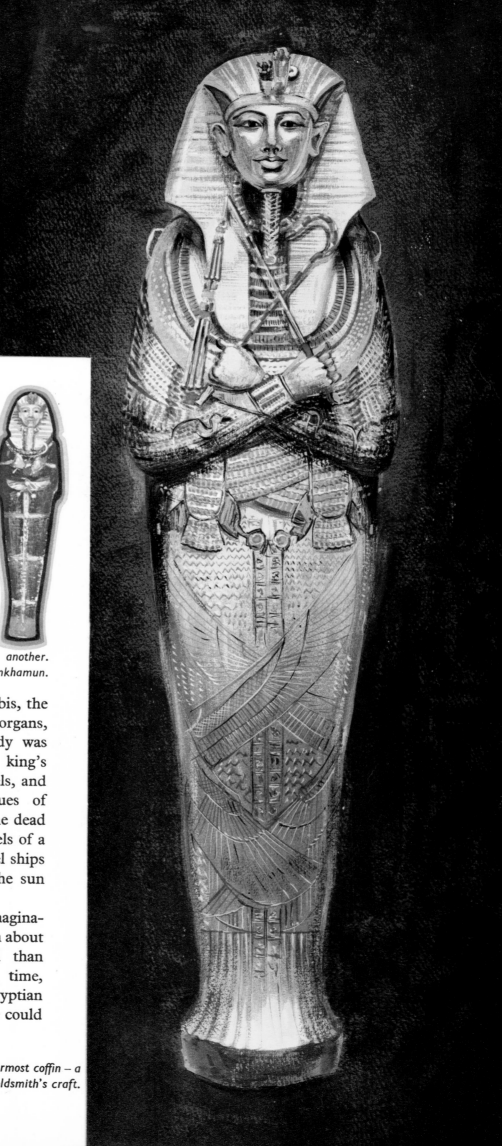

After piped steam thaws Alaskan mud, miners may find traces of primitive man.

Pueblo cliff-dwellings, over 800 years old, in Arizona.
James Fisher

Finds as spectacular as that of Tutankhamun's tomb are rare. More often the story of the past is built up from scattered fragments which, to the untrained eye, seem meaningless. From such scraps of evidence, discovered not only by excavators but also by other people who work close to the land, archaeologists have gleaned much knowledge about the early inhabitants of America.

The first Americans of all, we now think, came from Asia by way of the Bering Strait, perhaps as long ago as forty thousand years, when a land-bridge probably connected eastern Siberia and western Alaska. In both lands great deposits of bones of the same kinds of extinct animals have been found. In the frozen mud deposits of the Yukon Valley, in Alaska, gold-miners have also found, deep down in the soil, remains of extinct mammals associated with the flint points with which early hunters tipped their spears and arrows.

These primitive hunters were but the first arrivals. They were already men of modern type, for the earlier stages of man's development had taken place in the Old World. After them came others, some of whom, slowly and over centuries, made their way down the valleys and plains of

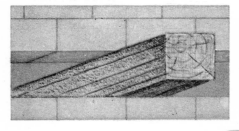

Annual growth-rings vary in thickness. A group near the outside of a sapling matches one near the middle of an older tree. A series of matching groups give a means of dating beams in ancient buildings.

North America, travelled through the narrow land-belt of Panama and eventually reached the southern continent. These men left their traces in many parts of the United States. In New Mexico, a negro cowboy found flint tools with the bones of an extinct type of bison. Tusks, marked by primitive hunters, have been discovered in Florida. Deep ploughing in Texas uncovered the bones of an American elephant, killed or wounded long ago by a stone spear-head.

In the New World, as in the Old, hunting was succeeded by farming, the foundation on which many widely differing civilisations were built. A great deal has been learned about the Mayas of Yucatan, the Aztecs of Mexico, the Incas of Peru, and the Pueblo people of the south-western United States who lived in cliff-dwellings and villages of stone; but so far we know little of the origins of these peoples or how each came to build up its own highly individual way of life. Nor is there yet much that is certain about the Vikings of the old Icelandic sagas who, during the tenth century, made almost unbelievable journeys across northern waters from Iceland and Greenland to the north-east of America.

It may well be that in North America discoveries as exciting as any yet made in the Old World still await the archaeologist. Meanwhile business concerns and private individuals, as well as professional archaeologists, are adding to our knowledge.

Not many years ago, workmen laying a new pipe-line for a natural gas company discovered a large

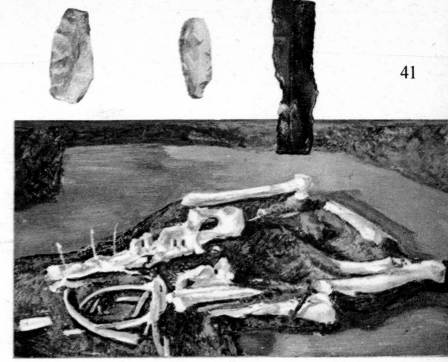

The tools and weapons of the early inhabitants of America are often unearthed together with the remains of extinct animals.

buried Pueblo village. Archaeologists, taken on the company's pay-roll, were able to make a proper excavation of the site.

Progress, too, is being made in dating antiquities. One method, developed in America, is called tree-ring dating. The thickness of growth-rings in a tree depends on weather conditions during the growing season. The ten rings of a ten-year-old tree vary in thickness just as the outer ten rings of one fifty years old. In the same way, the inner ten rings of the fifty-year-old match the outer ten of a still older tree. By matching up a chain of older and older trees it is possible to work out the age of timber used in ancient Indian buildings.

Mound built by unknown Indian tribe

A Pueblo dwelling which archaeologists later excavated (left) was revealed by pipe-liners working in the south-western States.
El Paso Natural Gas Company

At Byblos, north of Tyre, stand the remains of temples built long before that of Solomon.

At Jericho digging has revealed several buried cities.
Palestine Exploration Fund

Decorated

Finds in three continents

Throughout the world, archaeology is revealing ever more of man's buried past. In some areas it is concerned with pre-history; in others it is providing a background to historical events.

In the Near East, excavation adds constantly to our knowledge of the everyday life which lay behind the Bible stories. Wall-paintings, pieces of masonry, carvings in ivory, and metal furnishings dating back to the days of King Solomon, deepen our understanding of temple architecture and decoration at the time of this most famous of all temple-builders. At Byblos, north of Tyre, remains of temples more than a thousand years older than that of Solomon have been unearthed.

On the site of Jericho, the city which fell to the armies of Joshua, the remains of several ruined cities have been explored. One of the strangest of recent finds made there was that of human skulls, thought to be some seven thousand years old, on which features were modelled in plaster and shells inserted into the eye-sockets. Were these 'sculptures' trophies of war or were they tributes to ancestors? The answer is not yet known.

Chance played a part in one of the latest discoveries in this area of the world. For many years travellers have noticed strange carvings, often

Pottery of Old Testament times, found in a cave near Nazareth.
Oriental Institute, University of Chicago

showing hunting scenes, on rocks in the Negev Desert, in southern Israel. Until recently they were taken to be the work of modern Bedouin Arabs. A few years ago, members of a geographical expedition found that some of them were accompanied by inscriptions such as no modern Bedouin Arab would make. Archaeologists made further

Ancient carvings on rocks in the Negev Desert
Anati

investigations and discovered that these inscriptions were in four different languages. The earliest of the inscribed carvings date back to three hundred years before Christ; others, without inscriptions, may have been made much earlier.

The Treasure of Panagurishte, one of the most magnificent finds of recent years, was discovered by three brothers who were digging clay for bricks in southern Bulgaria. Nine vessels of solid gold were found buried seven feet deep in the ground. Some of the reliefs on these vessels, almost 2,500 years old, depict gods and heroes of ancient times. One shows Theseus who, according to legend, slew the Minotaur, the fabulous Cretan monster with the body of a man and the head of a bull.

Little more than a century ago, the interior of Africa was unexplored. Yet there, more perhaps than anywhere else, archaeology is now probing the earliest mysteries of man's development.

On the borders of Northern Rhodesia and Tanganyika, excavators recently examined the old beds of a lake which, because of changing rainfall through the ages, has altered its level several times. Buried at different levels were the tools of men who lived during the Early and Middle Stone Ages. A careful comparison of finds from five different levels helped to show how early man's stone tools gradually changed and improved.

One of nine gold vessels found by chance in southern Bulgaria.
National Museum, Plovdiv

On the border of N. Rhodesia, Stone-Age tools found at various levels show the development of craftsmanship.

Danes have rebuilt an Iron-Age house and arranged demonstrations of Iron-Age life

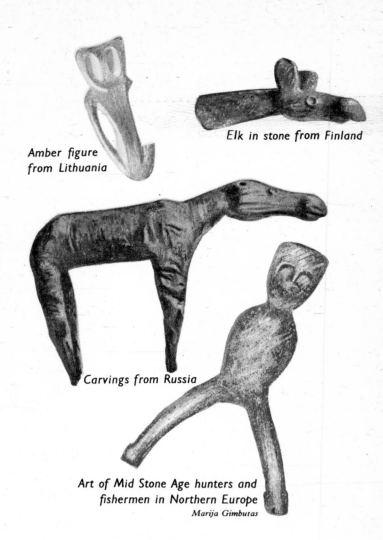

Amber figure from Lithuania

Elk in stone from Finland

Carvings from Russia

Art of Mid Stone Age hunters and fishermen in Northern Europe
Marija Gimbutas

IN NORTH-EASTERN Europe, also, archaeologists are constantly finding examples of early man's crafts. From Finland, Lithuania and northern Russia have come representations of human beings and more realistic carvings of animals in bone, wood, stone and amber. Many of these date back to between three and four thousand years ago when, in that area of the world, the Middle Stone Age was merging into the New Stone Age.

Today, however, archaeology goes much further than merely excavating and recording the traces of early man. Archaeologists have made films which vividly portray life in the Bronze Age. They have also reconstructed Iron Age houses and staged there demonstrations of how people lived and worked some two thousand years ago.

Tracking down the past is a process which goes on in all parts of the world. In the Altai Mountains of southern Siberia archaeologists have discovered burial chambers long filled with ice. More than two thousand years ago, tribesmen used this burial ground for their leaders and great men. Throughout the years the ice has wonderfully preserved not only the fully-clad bodies but also many of the treasures buried with them, including a carpet

which may well be the oldest pile carpet in the world. Its design, in common with that of several richly-figured wall-hangings, closely resembles those used in the Middle East, while the presence of silken goods indicates that these long-dead tribesmen of southern Siberia almost certainly had some contact with China.

Hundreds of tombs, some almost as old as those in the Altai Mountains, were discovered a few years ago while a reservoir was being constructed in central China. Wall-paintings and carvings found there give interesting glimpses of the life, costume and crafts of the time.

It was in China, too, that a clue from an unlikely source led to one of the most important discoveries of the present century. For many years Chinese apothecaries have sold crushed 'dragon bones' as a medicine. About 1900, German naturalists, studying quantities of these bones which they had bought in drug stores of the Far East, recognised them as the remains of extinct animals. Twenty years later, geologists began a search for their source. It was discovered that the bones came from a cave not far from Pekin, and with them

This prehistoric Siberian wall-hanging was evidently the work of a very fine craftsman.

What were 'dragon bones'?
Where did they come from?

Samples bought by German naturalists later led to a thorough investigation.

were found the fossil bones of many representatives of an extinct type of primitive man, together with weapons which he used for hunting and tools with which he dressed his meat.

The 'dragon bones' were the means of proving what was formerly unknown: that man must have lived in China in the exceedingly remote past.

Archaeologists examine a painting in a recently-excavated Chinese tomb.

They were traced to a cave near Pekin. They proved to be the fossil bones of . . .

. . . extinct animals, and of the earliest men yet known to have lived in East Asia.

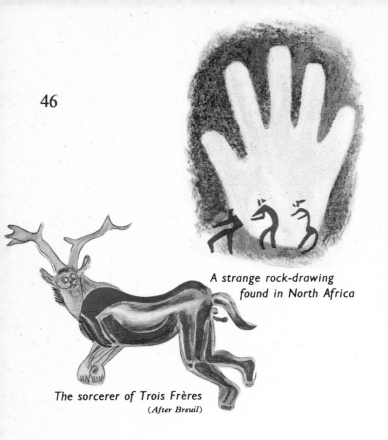

The sorcerer of Trois Frères
(After Breuil)

A strange rock-drawing found in North Africa

A superb example of early man's art, from the famous cave at Lascaux, in France.

Method and Science

WHAT ARE the techniques by which archaeology rounds out and pushes further back in time the story of mankind? As in other sciences, methods are all the time changing and improving. But two essentials remain: critical observation and extreme care in recording.

These qualities are outstanding in the long career of a great Frenchman, the Abbé Henri Breuil. By the age of twenty he was already familiar with the flint tools of the Old Stone Age and with a number of the caves which prehistoric men had once used as homes or as temporary shelters. It was the

spectacular rock-paintings and engravings in these caves which claimed more and more of the Abbé's interest and which were later to become the subject of his life's work.

In 1901, with other investigators, he visited the now-famous caves of Font de Gaume and Les Combarelles, in south-western France. Thanks to his tireless research, the superb paintings he saw there were for the first time recognised as examples of man's earliest pictorial art.

For many years the Abbé copied and traced primitive paintings and drawings, travelling widely

The Abbé Breuil has recorded hundreds of cave-paintings and engravings, often under considerable difficulties.

In painting friezes of this kind, the cave-artist used graphite, ochre and vegetable stains. Crushed twigs or a moss pad served as brush.
(After F. Windels)

in Europe, China, Ethiopia and, later, in South Africa. His careful and sensitive records were often obtained under conditions of almost unbelievable hardship. He spent nearly ten years in copying the engravings at Les Trois Frères, one of which alone is more than nine feet long.

It is mainly to the discovery and interpretation of the Abbé Breuil that we owe our knowledge of the first chapter of the history of art. Man's first pictures are chiefly concerned with animals – the mammoth, bison, ox, horse and reindeer which were the familiar quarry of the Old Stone Age hunters. The few human beings which appear are usually engaged in hunting or in ritual dances, or else are disguised in animal masks. From these associations there is little doubt that the pictures had a magic purpose: most probably they were intended to ensure success in the chase, for the cave-dwellers were dependent on hunting for their supplies of meat, hides, bones and fur.

Many cave-paintings display a combination of energy, animation and realism which only the best of our modern film-cartoonists achieve. Some – especially the simpler rock-drawings, like those shown in the margins of these two pages – also have the modern cartoonist's sparing use of line as well as his humorous touch.

When we realise how the cave-artist painted, we are struck by the wonder, as well as the beauty, of his work. He had no palette, no prepared paints, and no brushes. For his tints he used graphite, red and yellow ochre, vegetable stains and perhaps blood. The pigment was usually spread on as a fat-thickened paste, with crushed twigs, a moss pad, or the fingers, but sometimes it was blown on to the rock-surface as a powder.

The classical areas of cave art are the mountains of southern France and northern Spain. The best-known cave, at Lascaux in the Dordogne, was found in 1940 by schoolboys. There the French archaeologist, F. Windels, has used the camera to make worthy records of some of the most magnificent paintings produced by early man.

Today the camera is used in recording the paintings of long ago.

A composite picture of an area-excavation. On the left, surveyors and recorders are at work. A photographer is busy on the raised platform.

No matter how careful the archaeologist may be in observing and recording, his work will yield the best results only if he has a lively sympathy with the past and instinctively feels it as a reality.

It is not enough, for example, for him to be able to recognise and classify seventeen kinds of Saxon brooch: he must always be conscious that each was once pinned on a dress, that each could prick its owner's finger. Whatever advanced scientific techniques he may enlist in finding, preserving or dating antiquities, the archaeologist himself must provide that quality of thought and feeling which alone can span the time-interval between earlier people and those of our own age.

This is the firm belief of Sir Mortimer Wheeler, a leading British archaeologist and the most remark-

Strata beside a wall are shown by digging at right-angles to it.

able excavator since Pitt-Rivers. Apart from two intervals of distinguished military service, he has been digging up history for almost fifty years. His search for the past has taken him all over the world, from Roman Caerleon and Verulamium in Britain, to the hill-forts of Normandy and Brittany, to the sites of ancient settlements in the Indus valley and southern India, and to the Graeco-Roman trading stations on the east coast of Africa.

Sir Mortimer thus sums up the point and purpose of his long and fruitful work: 'We are not digging up things, but people.'

Fifty years ago he found archaeology an almost unorganised study. The remarkable change that has taken place since then is in no small measure due to his own mastery of technique, and to the importance he places on teaching it to others.

In the nineteen-thirties an Institute of Archaeology was founded in London, largely on Sir Mortimer Wheeler's initiative, for the training of students. Here was another great step forward. Almost for the first time it was realised that the careful methods practised by experienced archaeologists could be taught and later applied to almost any kind of archaeological problem. They could be used not merely in such places as Britain, which stood on the edge of the ancient world, but also in the areas where early civilisations reached their peak.

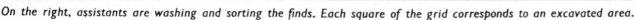

On the right, assistants are washing and sorting the finds. Each square of the grid corresponds to an excavated area.

Similar teaching institutions have now been founded in many other lands. Thus today, before the young archaeologist begins digging on an important site he is already well grounded in his profession. He understands the essentials of surveying, the various techniques of excavation, of sorting and classifying his finds; he knows just how and where photography can help him, when to call in a specialist in decipherment, what equipment to use in cleaning and preserving delicate ornaments before they are moved from a site.

He knows there is no one master-method of excavation, and that he must consider problems of each site as they arise. Where the site is known to have been inhabited, an area excavation based on a grid of squares is commonly used. Trial trenches are sometimes dug as a preliminary. Deep and wide trenches are used to test and reveal sequence of structures, especially in fortifications.

But there is another side to teaching. Most of today's leading archaeologists have never forgotten that the story of bygone times is our common heritage. In words that we can all understand, in books, by radio and by television, they bring the living past to our own firesides.

Perhaps Sir Mortimer Wheeler had this in mind when he said, 'Sweating with the pen is no less important than sweating with the spade.'

Indian archaeologists in deep-trench excavation at Harappa, in India.
Archaeological Survey of India

The Royal Cemetery at Ur. Here the techniques of preserving fragile objects on the spot were brilliantly successful.

First-aid in the field

Another great believer in the value of teaching and training is Sir Leonard Woolley, who between 1922 and 1934 directed the joint British and American expedition to Ur, home of some of the first anti-quaries. He knew that the area likely to yield the most important finds was the Royal Cemetery. Even with an accomplished archaeologist constantly supervising, the task of excavating so promising a site could not well be left to any but the most highly skilled diggers. Woolley therefore postponed work on the Cemetery for two years, meanwhile con-centrating on less vital areas where his assistants could more safely gain experience.

With a highly skilled team of workers and with very simple equipment, Woolley succeeded in preserving many valuable objects which, with a little less care, might easily have been destroyed. Antiquities which had suffered decay under the salt-laden soil of Ur were given 'first-aid treat-ment' on the spot, so that technical specialists in museum laboratories could later ensure their preservation or reconstruct them.

The story of Queen Shub-ad's sledge-chariot shows what remarkable results this sort of first-aid treatment can give. The first sign of this beautiful piece of furniture was a golden mask, in the shape of a lion's head, standing upright in the earth. Close by it were the loose fragments of a strip of mosaic in shell and lapis-lazuli. They were covered with melted wax and no attempt was made to move them until the wax had hardened, holding them firmly in

Gold lion-masks – first sign of a royal sledge-chariot.

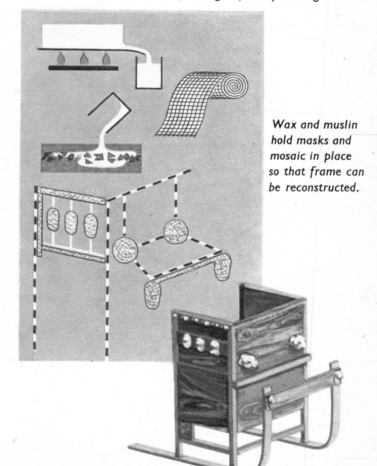

Wax and muslin hold masks and mosaic in place so that frame can be reconstructed.

Mud-caked inscribed tablets are baked hard before being cleaned.

of mosaic work, loose in the soil and scattered at various levels. The mounting on which they had once been fixed had perished. Here again careful first-aid was applied with wax and muslin. Patient and very detailed laboratory work followed. The result was the famous Standard of Ur, a banner of mosaic work made to be carried aloft on a pole, and decorated with priceless contemporary pictures of the Sumerian army.

Equally dramatic is the story which begins with the finding of two curiously-shaped holes in the ground. By filling them with liquid plaster, the excavators obtained a cast of a harp from the impression left by its decayed wooden framework.

Yet quite often preservation on the spot was little more than a dull, routine job. Inscribed clay tablets, caked with mud and softened by their long burial in the earth, were baked hard before any attempt was made to clean them. The fragile remains of human skeletons were treated with wax so that they could be moved just as they were found.

Such routine work, no less than the spectacular reconstructions, added their quota to our knowledge of the life, the written records and the burial customs of a past civilisation.

position; then the whole resulting strip was bound and reinforced with muslin. Further cautious digging uncovered more inlay work, which was treated in the same way, and more golden masks. At every stage of the work, notes of measurements were made and photographs taken, until it became clear that both masks and mosaic had once been fixed to a wooden framework that had long since rotted away. From the archaeologist's detailed records, a new framework was made; masks and mosaic were attached to it just as they had been to the original. In this way a complete reconstruction was built up.

On another occasion, away in one corner of a royal tomb, excavators uncovered other fragments

Liquid plaster, poured into two curiously-positioned holes in the ground and allowed to set hard, formed . . .

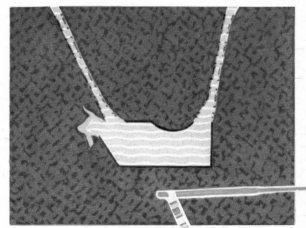

. . . the cast of an ancient harp, from which it was possible to make a complete reconstruction.

The fragile remains of human skeletons were treated with wax so that they could be moved intact.

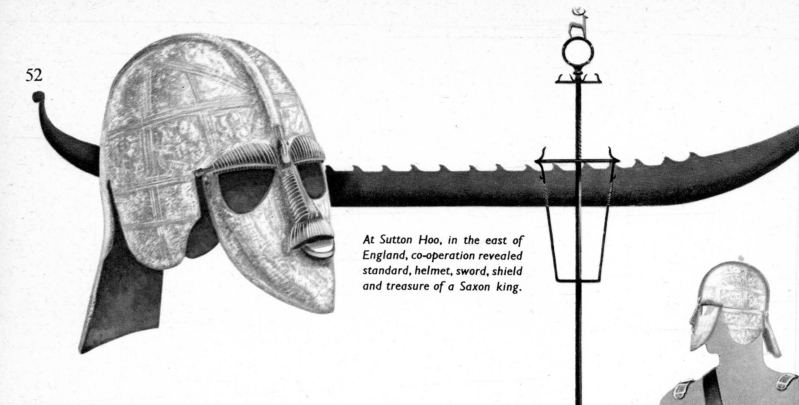

At Sutton Hoo, in the east of England, co-operation revealed standard, helmet, sword, shield and treasure of a Saxon king.

Team-work on a ghost ship

The rapid progress of archaeology during the present century is everywhere marked by fine team-work; and very often people whose interests lie in quite different directions are called upon to become members of the team. That is what happened in 1939 when the most amazing archaeological discovery yet known in Britain was made at Sutton Hoo, near the coast of Suffolk.

In Saxon times a great, open sea-going boat had been buried there in a trench dug in the sandy soil. In it, under a pent-roof like a Noah's Ark, were the magnificent treasures of a Saxon king: a bronze and iron helmet decorated in silver, a sceptre, silver bowls and dishes, garnet-set gold jewellery, and a standard of iron bearing at its head a life-like bronze model of a stag. Boat, treasure, and pent-roof were all buried under a mound, long since covered with vegetation.

During the late sixteenth century, robbers had dug a shaft in an attempt to find the treasure, but happily they had missed it. Not until the twentieth century was it to be revealed by the skill and co-operation of modern archaeology.

What kinds of people were involved in the work? First local archaeologists asked advice from the British Museum and from one of the large government departments – the Ministry of Works. Then professional archaeologists with special excavating experience took charge. A naval architect gave advice on the boat, a botanist on its timbers, and a soil-scientist on geological problems. The Ministry of Works lent special equipment. Expert photographers and draughtsmen recorded every stage of the excavation, during which police protection was given to the valuables. Cleaning, repair and restoration of weapons, jewellery, woodwork, bone, leather and textiles was undertaken by the scientists of the British Museum Laboratory.

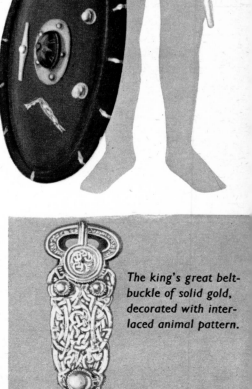

The king's great belt-buckle of solid gold, decorated with interlaced animal pattern.

The timbers of the burial ship had rotted away, leaving only nails and stains in the sand. Patient work laid bare the ghost of a ship.

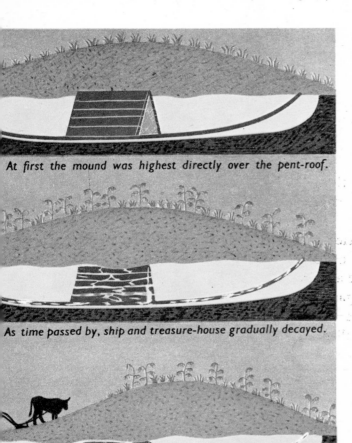

At first the mound was highest directly over the pent-roof.

As time passed by, ship and treasure-house gradually decayed.

That and work on the land changed the shape of the mound.

Grave-robbers dug in the top of the mound but missed the treasure. Modern excavators, with more careful work, found it.

The team not only unearthed a treasure worth more than a quarter of a million pounds sterling, but also revealed a valuable page of Saxon history. The strange memorial they uncovered was not a grave but a cenotaph, for no body was buried there. Yet forty gold coins give a clue to the king in whose memory it was made. They date the burial of the ship to a period between 650 and 670 A.D., during which two notable East Anglian kings died: Anna, in 654, and Aethelhere, killed in battle in 655.

Several of the dead king's valued possessions were heirlooms handed down from the days of the Norse sagas which had seen the origin of the royal house. Two silver spoons bearing, in Greek, the names Saul and Paul – reminders of St. Paul's conversion – were probably a present to mark the king's own conversion to Christianity.

A large collection of silver bowls, dishes and ladles of various dates, from Eastern Europe and the Middle East, indicate something of the trade connections of Saxon England. Among other finds were drinking horns and cauldrons, reminders of the feasting scenes in the Anglo-Saxon epic poem, *Beowulf*.

But the greatest triumph at Sutton Hoo was the investigation of the ship itself. The timbers had rotted away, leaving nothing but iron nails and stains in the sand. Patiently the unstained sand around them was carved and brushed away until the very ghost of a ship remained: ribs, strakes, gunwales were all outlined in the natural soil.

From this evidence the lines of a ship of the period were reconstructed. Team-work had given substance to a ghost and brought a piece of dead history to life.

The great ceremonial whetstone

Cretan inscribed tablet
(Zwemmer)

Some signs used in 'Linear B' script

Some of the most fascinating and tantalising problems of archaeology are those concerned with early forms of writing: fascinating because ancient documents may suddenly floodlight a dark corner of the past; tantalising because they may defy all attempts at decipherment for many years, as happened in the case of the inscribed clay tablets of ancient Crete.

Until the end of last century, little was known about the civilisations that flourished in Crete between three and five thousand years ago. Then in 1900, Sir Arthur Evans began his excavations on the site of the city of Knossos, during which he unearthed the vast and complex palace of the Cretan sea-kings, the famous Palace of Minos. At the peak of its grandeur, about 1400 B.C., the palace had contained throne-room, council chamber, workshops, huge magazines for the storage of wine and oil, and luxurious living quarters fitted with elaborate water-supply and

drainage systems. Beautiful wall-paintings, fine statues and carvings, even the decoration on gigantic storage-jars, all spoke of a high state of civilisation. Yet many hundreds of inscribed clay-tablets added nothing to our knowledge of ancient Crete until years after their discovery.

At various periods the ancient Cretans used three different scripts. The last-developed of these, in use just before the destruction of Knossos, and called 'Linear B', long defied all attempts at interpretation. In deciphering the scripts of Egypt, scholars had had the help of the Rosetta Stone. Here there was no such clue. How, then, was the problem to be tackled?

The answer was finally found by a young English architect, Michael Ventris. For years he worked patiently, both alone and with others, using many of the highly-technical systems of the trained cryptographers, or code-breakers. The fact that 'Linear B' consisted of about seventy common signs made him think that each stood for a different syllable, since several languages make use of about seventy syllables. The fact that similar inscriptions had been found on the Greek main-

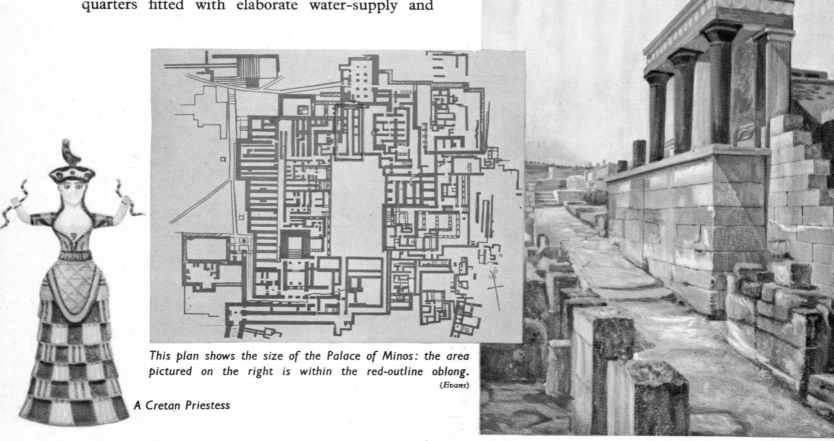

This plan shows the size of the Palace of Minos: the area pictured on the right is within the red-outline oblong.
(Evans)

A Cretan Priestess

This famous fresco shows a sport in which both the men and women of ancient Crete may have joined: somersaulting on the back of a bull.

(Evans)

land suggested that the language of Crete might have some connection with that of ancient Greece. Ventris examined hundreds of inscriptions, analysing how frequently the various signs occurred, noting how often they formed certain recognisable groups, watching for any clue that might hint at sound-values or meanings. In time he drew up a table giving to each sign a sound-value which occurred in ancient Greek. If his table were correct the inscriptions should now make sense.

He put theory to the test. Part of one inscription thus translated, read: 'Horse-vehicle, painted red, with bodywork fitted, supplied with reins.' This certainly made sense and so did many others. Ventris's feat of decipherment has been called 'The Everest of Greek archaeology'.

So far the inscriptions found have proved to be little more than lists of goods. But if the day comes when more of Crete's written history is unearthed, it will at once be plain to read.

One of the many giant jars which the Cretans used for storage.

Imagine a prehistoric food-storage pit. It serves its purpose, falls into disuse and collapses. By a natural process of silting, it gradually fills up until there is nothing to mark where it was. Many centuries pass by and the site becomes a field, yielding crops year after year. One spring it is sown with wheat. The soil in the disused pit, lighter in texture than that around it, holds moisture and encourages a fine growth of young wheat. From ground-level the difference in the quality of the crop may be scarcely visible, but from the air, the patch of more luxuriant growth is conspicuous, often with a characteristic shape of

Today the past yields up its secrets not only to the excavator digging down into the earth but also to the cameraman flying high above it. In Southern Europe and in Tunis, air photographs have added much to our understanding of prehistoric settlements, Etruscan tombs and Roman farms. In Scotland, a new air reconnaissance has increased our knowledge of that frontier area of the Roman Empire to such an extent that part of its history must now be written afresh.

How is it that the camera gives such a clear picture from the air of what is hardly noticeable from the ground? One answer lies in a peculiar property of the ground itself. Once soil has been disturbed it seldom settles to precisely the same compactness as the undisturbed soil around it.

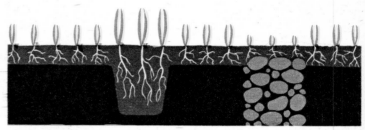

Above a disused pit, crops grow taller, but above masonry, shorter.

After the harvest an air-photograph shows only a plain field.

During early summer differences in luxuriance of growth among the young wheat crop show up, as lines, the buried walls of a Roman villa.
(After photographs by the late G. W. G. Allen, now in the Ashmolean Museum, Oxford)

its own. An air photograph tells the archaeologist that something of interest may lie beneath it.

Shallow soil, on the other hand, hinders growth by cramping roots and dispersing moisture. Buried structures such as roads and walls permit above them only areas of stunted growth which, especially during a drought, show on an air-photograph as lines and streaks.

Wheat, oats, barley and rye are helpful crops to the archaeologist; roots, woodland and scrub are useless. The nature of the sub-soil, too, is important. Differences in growth show up well in chalk or limestone, poorly in sand, clay or loose gravel. Season and quality of light must also be considered. It is useless to look for crop-marks after harvest, when only the stubble remains; spring, when growth has just begun, and summer when crops are ripe, are far better.

When the sun is low, irregularities in the ground-surface, even slight ones, cast quite long shadows. Air photographs taken at such a time often reveal features hardly visible to a ground-observer. Burial mounds, roadways and lost villages may then be recognised for the first time. What the camera reveals in outline, the excavator can later examine in detail.

Where part of a site has already been dug, an air-photograph may reveal a clear ground-plan and thus show where further digging would be likely to give the best results.

Shadows cast by ground irregularities reveal a medieval village.
(After photograph by J. K. S. St. Joseph)

When the sun is high, irregularities cast only short shadows. When the sun is low, shadows grow longer and can be seen from the air.

When viewed through a stereoscope, air-photographs will give a clear three-dimensional impression of the site.

El Amarna: air view records progress of excavation.
Egypt Exploration Society

58

Throughout the ages rocks and storms have taken toll of ships.

Occasionally the sea has yielded up relics to the nets of fishermen.

History from the sea-bed

Now free-divers seek them.

In studying the past, the archaeologist takes full advantage of every useful device the present can offer. When the Frenchman, Cousteau, developed the aqualung, archaeologists quickly seized on it as a means of plucking history from the sea-bed.

Throughout the ages, storms have taken toll of men's ships; at times, too, the sea has flooded whole towns. Occasionally the sea gave back some small relic to the hands of a sponge-diver or the net of a trawler. More rarely, tethered divers, taking their supply of air from above water, have fully explored a wreck, as in 1907 when French divers found a Greek galley, laden with works of art, which had sunk near Tunis two thousand years before.

Now free-diving opens up an exciting new field of archaeology. Along the south coast of France, off the shores of Italy, Spain and North Africa, divers equipped with masks, flippers and compressed air cylinders, constantly descend to the sea-bed to explore the remains of ships lost long ago. Pressurised cameras with flash-bulbs make graphic on-the-spot records; television cameras transmit up-to-the-minute news to the surface.

Already much has been learned of the wine trade of ancient Greece and Rome. Thousands of wine-jars, some with the inscribed wax seal of the shipper still in place, have been found. Occasionally the very timbers of the ship, lead plates from its bottom, and heavy anchors are recovered.

When a reconnaissance team discovers a submerged town, a large under-sea 'dig' begins. Plastic cord is used to mark off the site into squares, so that detailed records can be made of the position of each find. In the case of a ship buried in ooze, a large, flexible suction pipe clears away the overlying mud ready for the search to begin. Antiquities are often hauled to the surface in wire baskets.

This new technique is now practised beyond the confines of the Mediterranean, chief shipping route of the ancient world. In Lake Titicaca, between Bolivia and Peru, an American free-diver recently found the ruins of Chiopata, an ancient city of the Incas.

Reconnaissance team finds submerged building.

Divers square off the site with plastic cord.

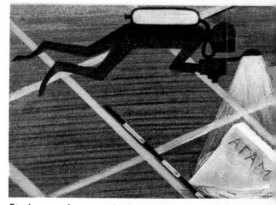
Finds are photographed and positions recorded.

Greek statue
found on sea-bed

Wire basket for
raising finds

Stamp on handle
of Greek wine-jar

Pressurised camera

High-power lamp

Suction-pipe for
clearing mud

Thick iron cabinet shields geiger counter from much of the radio-activity outside.

Screened counter

In some methods of radio-carbon dating, the sample is first reduced to a gas. Here is part of the apparatus used.

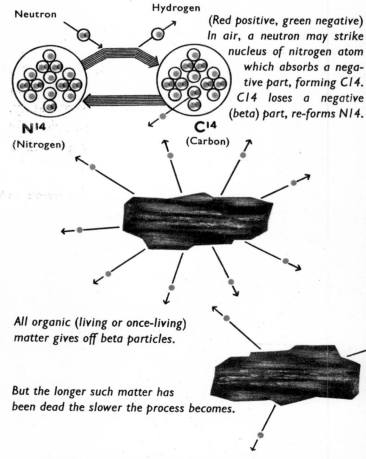

Neutron   Hydrogen

(Red positive, green negative) In air, a neutron may strike nucleus of nitrogen atom which absorbs a negative part, forming C14. C14 loses a negative (beta) part, re-forms N14.

N14 (Nitrogen)   C14 (Carbon)

All organic (living or once-living) matter gives off beta particles.

But the longer such matter has been dead the slower the process becomes.

One of the first questions that everyone asks the archaeologist is 'How old is it?' Atomic science has provided him with the most accurate answers.

Working at Chicago University, in the laboratories of the Institute of Nuclear Studies, Professor Willard F. Libby studied the formation of radio-active carbon in organic substances. He found that all plants, as they absorb carbon-dioxide from the air, take in with it minute quantities of a radio-active form of carbon known to scientists as Carbon-14. Since all animals depend directly or indirectly on plants for their food, it follows that every living thing contains Carbon-14. But when an organism, whether animal or vegetable, dies, it normally takes in no further carbon. Instead, its radio-active carbon begins to decay.

In dead organisms the proportion of Carbon-14 decreases at a fixed rate which does not vary under any known physical conditions. After 5,568 years, half the Carbon-14 content is lost; in the next 5,568 years half the remainder disappears, and so on. By comparing the amount left in any dead organic matter with the amount in living matter, scientists can estimate when the organism died.

The process, which is complicated and requires highly specialised apparatus, is still in an experimental stage both in America and Europe, but

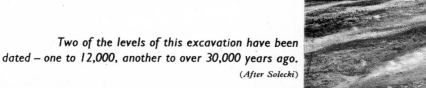

Two of the levels of this excavation have been dated — one to 12,000, another to over 30,000 years ago.

(After Solecki)

improvements are constantly being made. Briefly, suitable samples are first burned to form carbon-dioxide gas. In one method, the gas, after further chemical treatment, is then treated with magnesium to produce pure carbon. Finally the carbon, in the form of a paste, is fed to a geiger counter. The older the sample is, the less Carbon-14 it contains and the slower is the pulse of the geiger counter.

What sort of things have already been examined in this way, and what has this very modern technique taught us?

The shell of a land-snail from Jarmo, perhaps the oldest village in Western Asia, is found to be over 6,500 years old. Charcoal discovered in the entrance of the famous Lascaux Cave in France proves to be the remains of a fire which burned some 15,000 years ago. Trees killed by the last Ice Age in North America died about 11,500 years ago. Before carbon-dating began, geologists had thought that the last American Ice Age was much earlier.

Like every other archaeological method, radio-carbon dating still has limitations. Some kinds of organic material – and unfortunately bone is one of them – do not give such good results as others. Further, when organic material is much over twenty-five thousand years old, its Carbon-14 content is too small to be measured accurately. Yet despite limitations this wonderful new scientific aid will undoubtedly fill many of the gaps which still exist in the story of the remote past.

Courtesy Managers of Royal Institution
In this apparatus a flashing light shows 'pulse-rate' of sample under test.

Charcoal

The fire from which it came burned 15,000 years ago.
(After F. Windels)

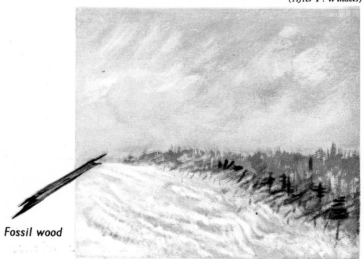

Fossil wood

From it we learn the date of America's last Ice Age.

Snail shells

These give clue to age of one of Asia's oldest villages.
Iraq-Jarmo Project, Oriental Institute, University of Chicago
C14 test tells when this extinct bison lived.

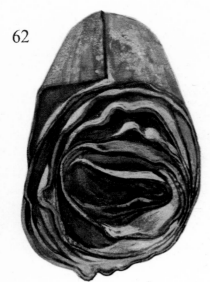

Bronze scroll from the Dead Sea: a brittle, corroded, complex mass.

On strips, writings were intact.

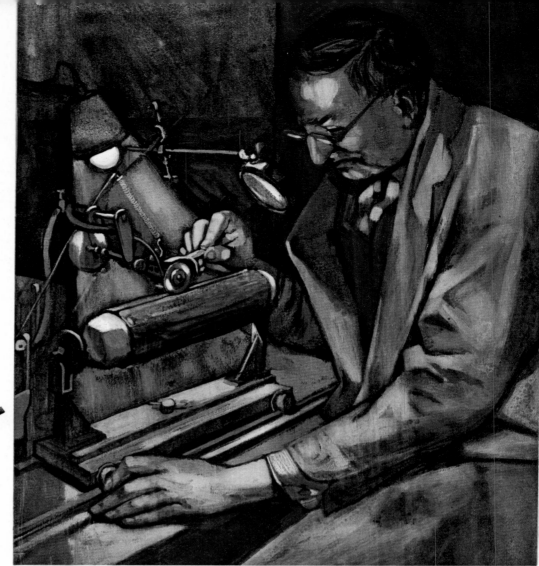

Scrolls were mounted on spindle, coated with adhesive to avoid crumbling, cut with special saw.

The geologist's knowledge of rock-formations gave a scale by which to measure past time.

It is not only nuclear physics which helps the archaeologist. Biology, botany, geology, chemistry are also revolutionising our approach to the past.

It was the geologist, with his specialised knowledge of various rocks and when they were formed, who first found a yardstick by which to measure past time. At first his scale, which measured time in millions of years, gave little help in dating the buried evidence of man, who has inhabited the earth for only a few hundred thousand years. But now the last part of the geologist's scale has been divided into very much smaller units. In Sweden, geologists have found that as glaciers partially melt each summer they leave behind a fine layer of sand or clay. These layers vary in thickness each year and, like the growth-rings in trees, provide a method of dating.

By identifying almost indestructible grains of fossil pollen, the botanist can tell what crops early man grew and even in what climatic conditions he grew them. The zoologist knows when various animals of past times lived and when they became

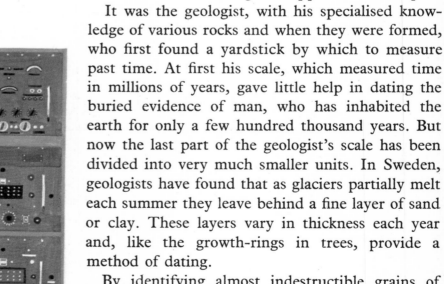

Control panel and X-ray tube of spectrographic-analysis apparatus.

When latex sets, it carries an exact copy of an inscription and can easily be peeled off.

Applying liquid latex to inscription on curved surface.

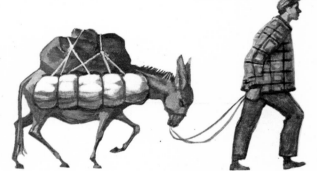

The 'squeeze' will survive rolling, folding and rough transport.

extinct. He can thus give a clue to the age of primitive weapons which are sometimes embedded in their remains.

Technical advances in many fields are enlisted in the work of archaeology. During the past few years a number of ancient written scrolls have been found near the Dead Sea. Two, made of bronze, had become extremely fragile because of the chemical changes they had undergone over many years. Any attempt at unrolling might well have destroyed them. Expert mechanical engineers mounted them on a spindle to avoid constant handling, coated the outside with strong adhesive to prevent crumbling, and used a special saw to cut them into slices. None of the uncorroded lettering was damaged.

Archaeologists have long used papier mâché to take 'squeezes' or impressions of inscriptions on old monuments. Now they can use liquid latex-rubber which, when it sets, gives a clearer impression, lasts longer, and is easier to move about.

Science provides the essential means of restoring and evaluating the genuine relics of early man; it also prevents the acceptance of false evidence.

The greatest forgery ever made in archaeology, the production in 1912 of the remains of Piltdown Man, once claimed to be 500,000 years old, was detected forty years later by the combined efforts of a whole team of scientists. Chemical tests proved that the skull contained much less fluorine than bones of that great age would normally contain. The presence of a chromium compound, used to give the bones the appearance of great age, was detected by X-ray spectrographic analysis. A close examination by expert anatomists suggested that the lower jaw was that of an ape.

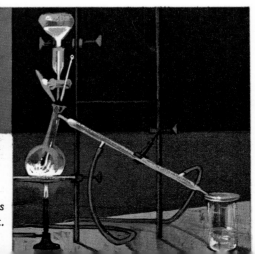

Jaw of 'Piltdown Man' (left) was like an ape's (right) but with flat teeth. Tests proved teeth were recently filed and one artificially 'packed'.

Real age of bones was detected by fluorine test.

The Past Has a Future

WITH ALL the aids of modern science at its disposal, what has archaeology achieved? Nowhere, perhaps, can we more clearly see the answer than in the great national museums. There the once-scattered pieces of bygone times are gathered together and arranged with such skill that the past comes to life before our eyes.

To make this possible, a great deal of work has gone on behind the scenes. Museum authorities organise archaeological expeditions to all parts of the world. In laboratories and workshops, finds which have received first-aid treatment in the field undergo further cleaning and repairing. From fragments which the excavator has unearthed and from the records and measurements he has made, skilled craftsmen prepare accurate reconstructions and models of antiquities which have suffered damage or decay. Every object is dated as closely as possible and subjected to the most rigid tests to prove its authenticity.

Skill in arrangement matches skill behind the scenes. No longer are Roman and Egyptian vases casually put with stuffed animals, as they were in so many ill-lit museums of last century. Finds are grouped according to period, place or culture, so that the group as a whole gives a clear picture of one aspect of man's history. Trained staff are always at hand to answer questions; specialists give every possible help in identifying antiquities brought in by visitors. There are conducted tours, lectures, demonstrations and film-shows.

Yet no museum, however big, can fully cover the archaeology of all times and all places, and some therefore specialise in the past of one or two areas. Smaller museums may even concentrate on the detailed archaeology of their own districts. But for students whose interests go beyond the displays, there are usually rooms set apart for quiet study and libraries containing a wide range of reference books. There are also museums attached to universities in which teaching is the main purpose.

Thus museums not only preserve and show to everyman the heritage of the past; they also help in the training of those who will some day set out to solve the mysteries which remain. For in spite of all that has already been achieved, there is no doubt that many exciting discoveries still await the archaeologist of the future.

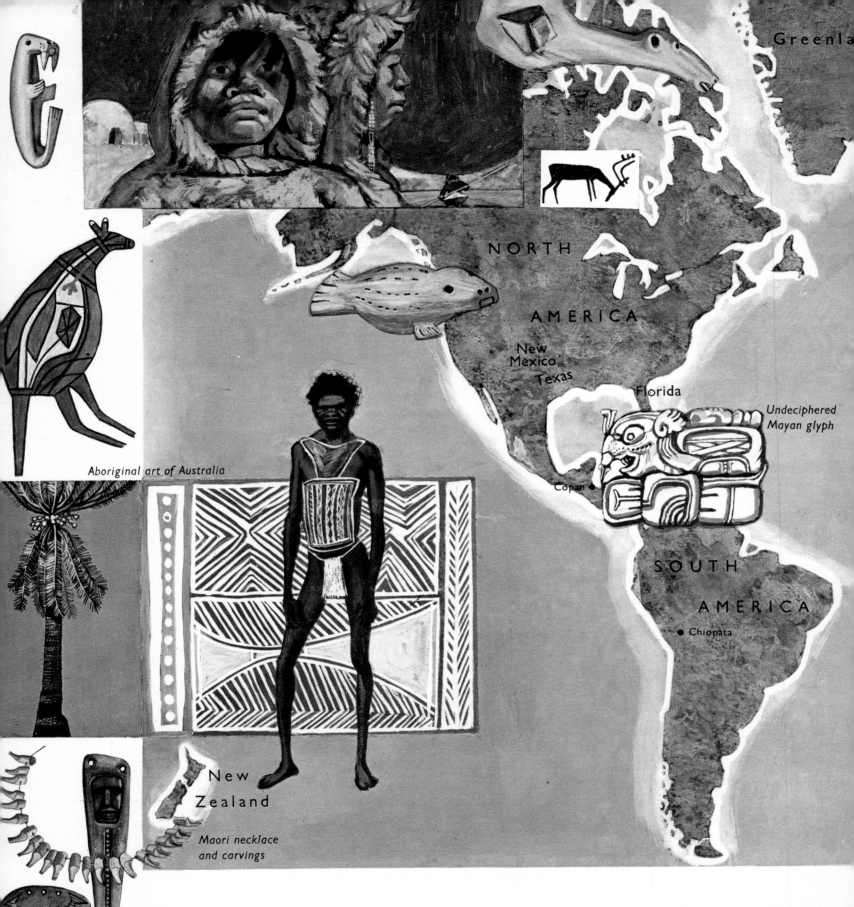

Aboriginal art of Australia

New Zealand

Maori necklace and carvings

Greenla

NORTH AMERICA

New Mexico
Texas

Florida

Copan ●

Undeciphered Mayan glyph

SOUTH AMERICA

● Chiopata

No-one has yet read the inscription on the Cretan Disc of Phaestos or learned the meaning of some of the strange glyphs of Central America. Archaeologists are still puzzled about the origin of certain prehistoric rock-paintings found in South Africa.

Secrets of the past are still hidden in the soil and in the sea. Many questions about early man's movements remain unanswered: Why did the Eskimos stay in Arctic lands while other early Americans migrated southwards? How did the aborigines of Australia, the Ainus of Japan, the

ASIA

Ainus

Altai Mountains

EUROPE

Sutton Hoo
Stonehenge

Lascaux

Trois Freres
Rome
Pompeii
Athens
Troy

Panagurishte

Byblos
Jericho
Babylon
Ur
El Amarna
Valley
of Kings

Benistun

AFRICA

Harappa

India

China

Pekin

Japan

Angkor

AUSTRALIA

early Maori settlers of New Zealand, come to develop their specialised tools and weapons, their highly individual arts and crafts?

The history of the last ten thousand years is fast unfolding, but further back man's story, as we see overleaf, is still largely lost in the mists of time.

Disc of Phaestos

*South African rock-painting –
'White Lady of Brandenburg'*

(After Breuil)

Unfinished Story

Early hunters in New Mexico by 17,000 B.C.

Cave artists
at work   23,000 B.C.

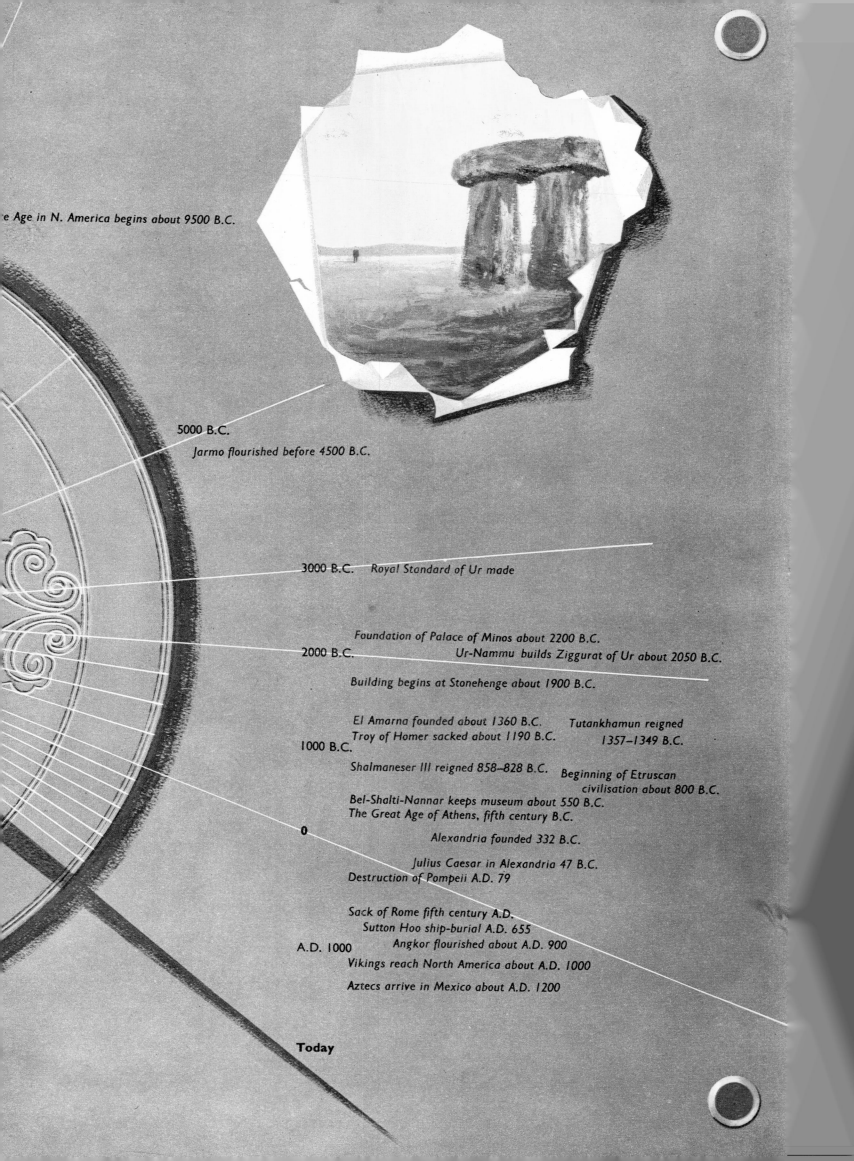

Age in N. America begins about 9500 B.C.

5000 B.C.

Jarmo flourished before 4500 B.C.

3000 B.C.   Royal Standard of Ur made

Foundation of Palace of Minos about 2200 B.C.

2000 B.C.   Ur-Nammu builds Ziggurat of Ur about 2050 B.C.

Building begins at Stonehenge about 1900 B.C.

El Amarna founded about 1360 B.C.   Tutankhamun reigned
Troy of Homer sacked about 1190 B.C.   1357–1349 B.C.

1000 B.C.

Shalmaneser III reigned 858–828 B.C.   Beginning of Etruscan
                                              civilisation about 800 B.C.

Bel-Shalti-Nannar keeps museum about 550 B.C.
The Great Age of Athens, fifth century B.C.

0   Alexandria founded 332 B.C.

Julius Caesar in Alexandria 47 B.C.
Destruction of Pompeii A.D. 79

Sack of Rome fifth century A.D.
Sutton Hoo ship-burial A.D. 655

A.D. 1000   Angkor flourished about A.D. 900

Vikings reach North America about A.D. 1000

Aztecs arrive in Mexico about A.D. 1200

Today